FIRST 100 DAYS OF DR. YUNUS
GOVERNMENT

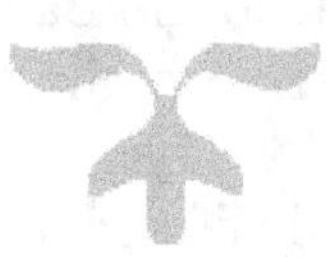

ABOUT THE AUTHOR

Dr. Dilip Nath is a distinguished leader in higher education and healthcare, known for his advocacy in voting's rights, Technology Justice & Human Right Defender. As a Harvard Kennedy School alumnus, he is celebrated for his transformative leadership.

With 30+ years of strategic planning expertise, Dilip focuses on using technology to bridge equity gaps in healthcare and education.

At 16, Dilip emigrated from Bangladesh to the US, becoming the first in his family to attend college. He lived in Queens for 34years, earning the trust of his community as a dedicated leader and activist.

Recognizing the importance of knowledge in politics, he embarked on a self-learning journey about US government and principles of democracy. He earned degrees from the State University of New York, including an MBA and a Doctorate in Business Administration (DBA).

Dilip is known for his visionary, team-oriented, and compassionate leadership. He is a respected advocate for various community issues, including healthcare, immigrant rights, and education. He founded NAVA and co-founded ABHF to further his endeavors.

DEDICATION

This book is dedicated to the freedom fighters, students, and brave individuals who have sacrificed their lives for democracy and equality in Bangladesh.

Your courage and pursuit of justice have laid a foundation for a nation built on freedom, equality, and human rights.

You exemplify heroism through selfless acts and unwavering commitment. Your bravery inspires generations, demonstrating determination and resilience.

We honor your sacrifices with gratitude and respect.

We support all religious minorities—Hindu, Buddhist, Christian, and others—in your fight for human rights and dignity in your own country.

PREFACE

100 DAYS OF CHANGE: THE YUNUS GOVERNMENT'S FIRST STEPS IN BANGLADESH

The first hundred days of any government are often regarded as a litmus test—a window into its priorities, policies, and the promises it seeks to fulfill. In the case of the Yunus-led government in Bangladesh, this period was more than just symbolic. It marked an unprecedented shift in the nation's political landscape, with a figure renowned for his social entrepreneurship and Nobel Peace Prize accolades stepping into the realm of governance—a realm often marred by entrenched power struggles, inefficiency, and corruption.

This book, not only chronicles those first hundred days, a period that ignited both hope and skepticism, but also chronicles background history of the independence of Bangladesh in 1971, and the aftermath of the ouster of the Prime Minister Sheikh Hasina on August 5, 2024. Upon going through, readers will have a complete understanding of the current state of affairs of Bangladesh.

August 8, 2024, Dr. Yunus took an oath as the head of the interim government after peoples' revolt against the then Prime Minister Sheikh Hasina's administration, mired in corruption, which raised hope, because Dr. Muhammad Yunus embodied a vision of innovation, inclusivity, and pragmatism that seemed capable of lifting Bangladesh to new heights. Skepticism, because political power has a way of eroding even the noblest intentions. Could an academic and social reformer navigate the murky waters of politics without compromising his ideals? Could a man celebrated for microfinance on a global stage tackle macro-level challenges like poverty, education reform, and institutional corruption within such a compressed timeframe?

Through these pages, the author(s) delve into the heart of those questions. Drawing from firsthand accounts, policy analyses, and the perspectives of ordinary citizens, we explore how the Yunus government redefined leadership during its critical early days. The narrative captures both triumphs and missteps, highlighting the tension between aspiration and implementation.

Dr. Yunus' ascendancy to power came at a time when Bangladesh stood at a crossroads. Years of political corruption, gridlock, social inequities, religious fundamentalism, and environmental vulnerabilities had left the nation yearning for change. Yet change, as history teaches us, is rarely linear. This book does not shy away from discussing the criticisms, challenges, and compromises that defined those early days. It does not seek to deify or vilify but to document a pivotal moment in Bangladesh's political history with clarity and nuance.

Readers will find here a story of transformation— not a completed journey but the opening act of a bold experiment in governance. Whether the Yunus government fulfilled its promises or fell short, these hundred days left an indelible mark, sparking debates about what leadership and accountability should mean in the 21st century.

As you turn these pages, consider not just the actions of one man or one administration, but the resilience and expectations of a people who dared to dream of a better tomorrow. In these stories of struggle and progress, you may find reflections and disappointments of your own hopes—for Bangladesh and for the universal pursuit of equity and justice.

This is a well written thought provoking book. After going through pages, readers will find out if peoples' expectations of corruption free society, equal justice, equal opportunity and treatment for all, including religious and ethnic minorities are met or not.

In the end, I am extremely delighted to write a preface for a time sensitive book about the first 100 days of Dr. Yunus Administration, which is a beginning, not the ending of a new chapter in Bangladesh.

I want to thank the Author(s) for giving me the opportunity for this write up.

Jitendra N. Roy, Ph.D., DABR,
Writer, Professor, Research Scientist & a Human Rights Activist.

TABLE OF CONTENTS

INTRODUCTION

PURPOSE AND SCOPE OF THE REPORT

Transitional politics reflects the strengths and weaknesses of nations, particularly as they navigate the growth of democracy. This book analyzes a major political upheaval in Bangladesh when Sheikh Hasina was ousted after 16 years in power, and Dr. Muhammad Yunus stepped in as the interim premier. The primary goal is to examine Dr. Yunus's initial actions in government, including his policies, the socio-political environment he entered, and the economic and global impacts of his leadership.

The emergence of social business, a model pioneered by Dr. Yunus, comes at a pivotal moment for Bangladesh. Some embraced his transition from Nobel Prize-winning economist to political leader, while others criticized it. While some viewed him as a mediator capable of bridging divides in a polarized nation, others doubted his governance abilities and accused him of being influenced by foreign powers. This report addresses these contrasting views by exploring key questions: How did Yunus rise to power? What structural and social changes characterized his early days in office? And what could Bangladesh's future look like under his governance?

Although this analysis does not focus solely on the current crisis, it examines the historical and socio-political context of Bangladesh. To understand the significance of Dr. Yunus's interim government, this work delves into the country's previous governmental systems, the causes of social and political unrest, the role of external forces, and internal rebellions. This multi-dimensional approach aims to shed light on not just what has happened but why it is relevant for the region and the world.

CONTEXT OF RECENT POLITICAL SHIFTS

Sheikh Hasina's ouster marks a significant turning point in Bangladesh's political history. From 2009 onward, Hasina led Bangladesh to economic growth, setting new GDP records and implementing the Vision 2021 project. However, her administration faced growing criticism for signs of authoritarianism. Many political challenges during Hasina's tenure stemmed from her leadership decisions, including the abolition of the caretaker government provision in 2011, which antagonized opposition parties, particularly the Bangladesh Nationalist Party (BNP), and fueled election controversies in subsequent years (Shehabuddin, 2024; The Britannica, 2024).

Dissatisfaction with Hasina's rule grew over time, culminating in 2024 when students launched the quota movement, initially demanding equal civil service employment opportunities for the underprivileged. Within months, this movement expanded into a nationwide protest against corruption, unemployment, and political injustice. These domestic protests, combined with international pressure and allegations of external influence, created a power vacuum that allowed Dr. Yunus to position himself as an interim leader.

The political shift raises questions about domestic discontent and broader global dynamics. Some suggest that Western actors funded the uprising, citing human rights violations and declining democracy under Hasina's rule, as reported by Asia-Pacific Research (2024). Critics argue that this interference aligns with broader geopolitical trends, such as countering Chinese influence in South Asia.

Opponents of Dr. Yunus contend that the West favored him as an internationally renowned and well-connected figure capable of stabilizing Bangladesh while advancing Western interests. However, Yunus's first 100 days in office have revealed significant challenges. His tenure has been marked by sectarian violence, economic instability, and labor rights abuses. Critics point to his nationalist and autocratic approach, including actions like disbanding opposition parties and empowering radical Islamist factions, as evidence of democratic decline in the country (BHBCUC, 2024).

This book acknowledges the dualism at play, analyzing Yunus's policies while considering the socio-political factors that led to his rise. It seeks to contribute to broader discussions on governance, democracy, and stability in South Asia.

CHAPTER ONE

HISTORICAL BACKGROUND OF BANGLADESH

INDEPENDENCE AND LIBERATION WAR (1971)

The independence of Bangladesh is one of the most historic and revolutionary events in the contemporary history of South Asia. Bangladesh emerged as a nation through a systematic genocide rooted in the prima facie discrimination faced by Bengalis in general and East Pakistan in particular. Following the partition of British India in 1947, Pakistan was divided into two regions separated by approximately 1,600 kilometers of Indian territory. Although East Pakistan (modern-day Bangladesh) was more populous, it was politically and economically dominated by West Pakistan, where the centers of political power, the military, and foreign exchange earnings were concentrated (Shehabuddin, 2024; Maniruzzaman, 1975).

BACKGROUND OF THE LIBERATION STRUGGLE

Income disparities between East and West Pakistan were a principal cause of the conflict. While East Pakistan contributed significantly to Pakistan's export earnings, primarily through the jute crop, development funds were disproportionately allocated to West Pakistan. For instance, during the first three five-year plans (1955–1970), only 25% of total development expenditures were allocated to East Pakistan, despite it being home to over 50% of the population (Shehabuddin, 2024).

In addition to economic inequality, East Pakistanis faced political marginalization. Key decision-making positions in administration, military, and planning were overwhelmingly occupied by West Pakistanis. These inequalities led to growing demands for decentralization and autonomy, culminating in the Six-Point Program articulated by Sheikh Mujibur Rahman, leader of the Awami League, in 1966 (Jahan, 1974; Britannica, 2024).

The growing dissatisfaction was most evident during the 1970 general elections. The Awami League, led by Mujibur Rahman, won all but two National Assembly seats out of 169 allocated to East Pakistan, securing a clear majority of 167 seats in the 313-member parliament. However, the ruling West Pakistani elite, led by General Yahya Khan and Zulfikar Ali Bhutto, refused to cede power. This decision triggered widespread civil unrest and strikes across East Pakistan.

Mujibur Rahman advocated for democracy and non-violent civil disobedience, garnering immense public support. However, the West Pakistani military's brutal and repressive actions escalated tensions, paving the way for the Liberation War (Maniruzzaman, 1975; Shehabuddin, 2024).

THE ONSET OF WAR

On March 25, 1971, the Pakistani military launched "Operation Searchlight," an assault on Dhaka aimed at suppressing the autonomy movement. This operation targeted students, political activists, and intellectuals, resulting in thousands of deaths. It marked the beginning of a nine-month-long liberation war, characterized by widespread human rights abuses. Estimates suggest that between 300,000 and 3 million civilians were killed, while around 10 million fled to India, creating one of the largest refugee crises in history and a major humanitarian disaster (Shehabuddin, 2024; Encyclopedia Britannica, 2024).

The violence extended to women, with systematic sexual violence and forced abductions committed on a massive scale. It is estimated that over 200,000 women were raped during the conflict, highlighting the brutal atrocities perpetrated by the Pakistani Army (Shehabuddin, 2024; BHBCUC, 2024). Additionally, religious minorities, particularly Hindus, were targeted with mass killings and expulsions from their villages. These traumatic events remain deeply ingrained in the Bengali psyche and continue to shape socio-political discourse in Bangladesh to this day (Maniruzzaman, 1975).

INDIA'S ROLE AND THE EMERGENCE OF BANGLADESH

India played a pivotal role in the liberation of Bangladesh. During the humanitarian crisis, India provided the Mukti Bahini (Bangladeshi freedom fighters) with training, equipment, and financial support. The escalating border tensions and the influx of refugees compelled India to intervene militarily. On December 3, 1971, the Indo-Pak War began, lasting 13 days. On December 16, 1971, Pakistan surrendered, leading to Bangladesh's recognition as a sovereign state (Shehabuddin, 2024; Britannica, 2024).

The emergence of this new state came with numerous challenges for its leadership. Despite achieving independence, the war left Bangladesh with widespread destruction of infrastructure, loss of lives, and displacement of populations. However, the struggle fostered a profound sense of national pride and unity, as the people of Bangladesh recognized the immense sacrifices made for their sovereignty.

CHALLENGES OF NATION-BUILDING (1972–75)

The immediate post-independence period under Sheikh Mujibur Rahman, known as "Bangabandhu" (Friend of Bengal), was marked by both progress and setbacks. Bangladesh faced severe poverty, famine, and the destruction of physical infrastructure. The economy was devastated, with industries, transport systems, and public services severely impacted. In 1972, per capita income was below $100, placing Bangladesh among the poorest nations in the world (Jahan, 1974; Shehabuddin, 2024).

ECONOMIC RECONSTRUCTION AND SOCIALIST POLICIES

To address these challenges, Sheikh Mujibur Rahman's government adopted socialist policies, emphasizing state-dominated industries, businesses, and banking sectors. Nationalization was introduced to revive industries and promote equitable wealth creation. However, these policies faced significant obstacles, including bureaucratic inefficiencies, corruption, and a lack of skilled professionals.

Political unrest, inadequate transportation infrastructure, and limited facilities further deterred foreign investment. Agricultural recovery was sluggish and compounded by natural disasters, including floods in 1974 and a famine. Food shortages and skyrocketing inflation eroded public confidence in the government.

Additionally, securing international aid proved challenging. The Cold War dynamics strained relations between Mujibur's government and Western donors, further hindering recovery efforts (Shehabuddin, 2024).

POLITICAL INSTABILITY AND THE RAKKHI BAHINI

Sheikh Mujibur Rahman initially sought to establish a parliamentary democracy. However, factionalism within the Awami League soon emerged, leading to the formation of a parallel group. Additionally, opposition from leftist and Islamist factions posed significant challenges. In response, the government created the Rakkhi Bahini, a paramilitary force tasked with maintaining order in the country. However, allegations of human rights abuses, such as arbitrary detentions and excessive use of force, tarnished its reputation and further undermined public confidence in the government (Maniruzzaman, 1975).

Amid growing public dissatisfaction, Mujibur declared a state of emergency in 1974. The following year, he abolished the multi-party political system and introduced the Bangladesh Krishak Sramik Awami League (BAKSAL), effectively establishing a one-party state. Mujibur justified this move as necessary for building a unified nation-state and achieving progress. However, it was widely viewed as authoritarian, sparking anger among key political constituencies, colleagues, and other politically affiliated groups. The decision deepened societal divisions and further alienated various segments of the population (Shehabuddin, 2024).

THE ASSASSINATION OF SHEIKH MUJIBUR RAHMAN

On August 15, 1975, a coup led by junior military officers resulted in the assassination of Sheikh Mujibur Rahman and most of his family members. This tragic event marked the end of Bangladesh's initial experiment with democracy and the beginning of years of direct military rule. The coup was followed by a series of political upheavals, as successive governments struggled to establish their authority amid a turbulent political landscape (Maniruzzaman, 1975; Shehabuddin, 2024).

The assassination of Mujibur Rahman is one of the darkest chapters in Bangladesh's history. It underscored the fragility of its early democratic institutions and highlighted the challenges of postcolonial nation-building. Economic difficulties, political divisions, and external pressures shaped the governance of this period. The impact of these events continues to influence the political culture of Bangladesh to this day. Despite its tragic end, this period holds valuable lessons for political activists about the complexities and sacrifices involved in nation-building.

CHAPTER TWO

CHRONOLOGY OF REGIME CHANGES (1975–2024)

MILITARY DOMINANCE (1975–1990)

The coup of August 15, 1975, which resulted in the assassination of Sheikh Mujibur Rahman, marked the end of Bangladesh's initial democratic experiment. Mujibur, his wife, son's, daughter-in-laws and several relatives were killed by junior military officers, creating a political vacuum that was subsequently filled by a succession of military leaders through coups and counter-coups. The first significant military figure to assume power in this volatile period was Ziaur Rahman, a former freedom fighter and army officer, who rose to power in the late 1970s (Maniruzzaman, 1975).

ZIAUR RAHMAN'S RULE (1975–1981)

Ziaur Rahman ascended to leadership following a counter-coup in November 1975. His administration brought significant constitutional and policy changes, the most prominent being the introduction of Islamic principles into Bangladesh's governance. Zia's government revised the 1972 Constitution to include "absolute trust and faith in Almighty Allah" in its preamble, effectively removing secularism as a state principle (Shehabuddin, 2024).

Zia also introduced political pluralism, allowing the formation of opposition parties. In 1978, he founded the Bangladesh Nationalist Party (BNP) to provide political support for his administration. Economically, Zia focused on privatization and liberalization, promoting the private sector to spur development. While these policies laid the foundation for economic diversification, they were criticized for fostering a system of crony capitalism, where benefits were distributed based on political favoritism rather than efficiency (Maniruzzaman, 1975).

Ziaur Rahman's rule ended abruptly when he was assassinated in an attempted coup on May 17, 1981, during an air raid. His death intensified rivalries within the military, leading to a period of instability. This turmoil provided General Hussain Muhammad Ershad with an opportunity to seize power and establish his regime across the country (Britannica, 2024).

HUSSAIN MUHAMMAD ERSHAD'S RULE (1982–1990)

Army General Hussain Muhammad Ershad seized power without any violence in 1982 by removing

the civilian government of President Abdus Sattar. Similar to his colleague M. Ershad aimed at Islamization of the state. He officially declared Islam as the state religion in 1988 which incidentally cemented religion fare deeper into the politics of Bangladesh(Shehabuddin, 2024).
In regards to political system, the regimes of Ershad were authoritarian systems. He also banned newspapers and closed down any political opposition, and often called on the military to support him. Nevertheless, more people are supporting Ershad because of his emphasis on development projects such as road, bridges, irrigations which are basically essential for agricultural people of the country (Maniruzzaman, 1975).

Criticism of Ershad's regime was mounting throughout the late 1980s in response to charges of corruption, fraud in the elections and overall violation of human rights. Protests spread throughout the country by 1990 when a combination of opposition parties and student organizations prompted Ershad to step down. Such actions indicated that the military no longer had control over Bangladesh politics as it was seen in the past the man's departure helped Bangladesh bd transition to democracy (Britannica, 2024).

DEMOCRATIC ERA AND ALTERNATING LEADERSHIP (1991–2024)

Since the general elections of 1991 which were held with a neutral care taker government Bangladesh has witnessed new phase in its political journey. In these elections, peoples' representatives were elected for their parliaments; thereby parliamentary democracy was restored and for the first time in more than a decade a civilian government headed by a leader named Khaleda Zia of BNP was formed (Shehabuddin, 2024).

KHALEDA ZIA AND THE BNP (1991–1996)

Under Khaleda Zia's administration, Bangladesh adopted policies aimed at economic liberalization, including the privatization of state-owned enterprises and efforts to attract foreign investment. However, her government was widely criticized for its failure to tackle corruption and political violence. Additionally, Khaleda Zia's regime was often accused of being intolerant of opposition voices, leading to a deeply polarized political landscape.

The rivalry between the BNP and Sheikh Hasina's Awami League intensified during this period, resulting in frequent strikes and protests. In 1996, the Awami League boycotted the elections, raising concerns about the credibility of the electoral process. The ensuing political crisis forced Khaleda Zia to relinquish power, leading to the establishment of a caretaker government tasked with conducting fresh elections (Britannica, 2024; Shehabuddin, 2024).

SHEIKH HASINA AND THE AWAMI LEAGUE (1996–2001)

Sheikh Hasina became the Prime Minister of Bangladesh for the first time after her party, the Awami League, won the 1996 elections. Her tenure was marked by several landmark achievements, including the signing of the Ganges Water Sharing Treaty with India and the establishment of the International Crimes Tribunal to prosecute those involved in the 1971 Liberation War genocide.

Despite these accomplishments, her government faced criticism for alleged corruption and inefficiency. These accusations were capitalized on by the BNP in the lead-up to the 2001 elections, contributing to the Awami League's electoral defeat (Britannica, 2024).

POLARIZATION AND POLITICAL STALEMATE

Between 2001 and 2008, Bangladesh witnessed heightened political polarization. The BNP and the Awami League, the two dominant political parties, engaged in undemocratic practices, further eroding public trust in the political system.

The caretaker government system, initially introduced to ensure impartiality in elections, began losing credibility. Sheikh Hasina's government repealed the caretaker system in 2011, justifying it as a constitutional necessity. However, this move drew widespread protests and allegations of authoritarianism. The period also saw increasing tensions between political activists and security forces, contributing to a broader climate of instability (Asia-Pacific Research, 2024).

SHEIKH HASINA'S 16-YEAR RULE (2009–2024)

Sheikh Hasina Wazed, daughter of Bangladesh's founding leader Sheikh Mujibur Rahman, has played a pivotal role in the country's political and economic transformation. Taking over the leadership of the Awami League in 1981, Sheikh Hasina eventually emerged as one of South Asia's most prominent leaders. Her tenure as Prime Minister from 1996 to 2001 set the stage for Bangladesh's growth, but her successive rule from 2009 to 2024 witnessed the country's most transformative years.

Sheikh Hasina Wazed assumed the chairmanship of the Awami League, the political organization founded by her father, in 1981. This marked the beginning of her political career, and she went on to become one of the most influential and powerful figures on the global stage.

From 1996 to 2001, Sheikh Hasina served as Bangladesh's first Female Prime Minister, during which the country's economy experienced remarkable improvement. Despite this economic growth, poverty remained a significant issue, and reducing poverty became a primary focus of her administration. With a GDP growth rate of approximately 7% per year for much of her tenure, she was re-elected as Prime Minister in 2009, holding office until August 2024, when she was ousted. She is recognized as a vocal advocate for democracy and human rights in Bangladesh, playing a crucial role in regional politics and contributing to peace and stability in South Asia. Sheikh Hasina's complex and contentious nature has made her one of the most prominent leaders in the region.

Additionally, Sheikh Hasina was awarded the Houphouet-Boigny Peace Prize by UNESCO in 1998 for her efforts in ending the Chittagong Hill Tracts War, which lasted 25 years. Despite this achievement, many critics accuse her of imposing tougher restrictions on press freedom, claiming she used autocratic power over her detractors. On the other hand, Hasina has consistently highlighted Bangladesh's exceptional economic achievements throughout her tenure (International Desk, 2023). During her time in office, Bangladesh's GDP per capita quadrupled, and the country saw unprecedented economic growth. Her primary goal has been to eradicate poverty, and the number of people living below the national poverty line has been reduced by more than half. She has also expanded access to healthcare and education, and made significant investments in infrastructure.

RISE AND FALL

Bangladesh has made tremendous progress in several areas, including infrastructure, health, and education. As a result, the country now enjoys greater overall wealth and significantly reduced poverty. This is especially important given that Bangladesh was one of the poorest countries in South Asia at the time of its independence. Bangladesh has become a unique case in economic development, with sustained GDP growth (outpacing neighboring Pakistan) and its status as one of the fastest-growing economies in the world. Since 2000, the average annual GDP growth has increased by 6.8%. The percentage of people living in poverty has decreased from 43% in 1991 to 20% in 2023. Bangladesh has achieved universal primary education completion and is on track to achieve universal secondary education completion by 2030. The country has also made significant strides in improving maternal health and reducing child mortality.

Although Bangladesh has made rapid economic progress in recent years, its political development has been more challenging. Particularly in the aftermath of the December 2018 legislative elections, the country has come under increasing pressure to abandon its commitment to democracy, the rule of law, and human rights. Concerns have been raised about the impartiality and transparency of the voting process, prompting a review of the country's political institutions. The parliamentary elections in December 2018 were marred by allegations of vote-rigging and intimidation. The Election Commission was accused of being biased in favor of the incumbent party (The Economist, 2023).

In January 2024, Sheikh Hasina secured her fifth term in office. Although the Bangladesh Nationalist Party (BNP) and its allies boycotted the election, 27 out of 44 registered parties participated, alongside nearly 1,900 independent candidates competing for 300 parliamentary seats. Despite BNP's absence, meaningful multiparty competition occurred. However, concerns persist that Bangladesh may be moving toward one-party rule under the Awami League (AL).

Despite challenges in economic and political governance, Bangladesh has made substantial progress in terms of social development indicators. Achieving targeted health outcomes, however, remains closely tied to governance challenges. The government aspires to achieve "Digital Bangladesh" by 2021, but there are significant impediments to realizing this goal. Bangladesh's local government system has seen minimal development in terms of efficiency, power decentralization, democratic practices, and public participation. Despite these hurdles, Sheikh Hasina has remained committed to promoting macroeconomic stability and investing in human capital, yielding positive outcomes and improving Bangladesh's overall economic trajectory. Furthermore, Bangladesh has taken a strong stance on the international stage by advocating for the achievement of the Sustainable Development Goals (SDGs), with a focus on climate change adaptation and mitigation, effective use of water resources, aid efficacy, and the promotion of female education (Tribune Report, 2023).

Bangladesh has seen significant improvements in various sectors under the leadership of Sheikh Hasina. These changes include:

❖ **Poverty Reduction:** Under Sheikh Hasina's leadership, poverty reduction has been a major focus, and as a result, Bangladesh's poverty rate has dramatically decreased. According to World Bank data, poverty in Bangladesh declined from 31.5% in 2010 to 24.3% in 2016. To achieve this, the government has implemented a variety of policies, including job creation, microfinance programs, and social safety nets.

❖ **Economic Progress:** Under Sheikh Hasina's administration, Bangladesh has made remarkable economic progress. Over the past 10 years, the nation's GDP has expanded by an average of 6% per year. Contributing factors to this growth include the expansion of the garment industry, the development of infrastructure, and the growth of the services sector.

❖ **Improved Living Conditions:** Sheikh Hasina's administration has prioritized improving the standard of living for all citizens. Healthcare, education, and housing have all benefited from increased investment. For instance, the government's Ashrayan initiative aims to create over 4 million low-income housing units.

❖ **International Recognition:** Sheikh Hasina's leadership has received global recognition. In 2020, she was awarded the prestigious Gandhi Peace Prize for her advocacy of nonviolence and other Gandhian methods of social, economic, and political development.

In conclusion, under Sheikh Hasina's leadership, Bangladesh has experienced tremendous improvements, including a reduction in poverty, significant economic progress, improved living standards, and global recognition. She remains a powerful leader due to her unwavering commitment to her country's progress and her strong support for Least Developed Countries (LDCs) on the world stage.

POLITICAL UPHEAVAL IN 2024

It may also be mentioned that the dissatisfaction process gradually emerged and culminated during Hasina's rule in the 'student quota movement' and various protests in 2024. This unrest together with allegations of outside influence led to her ouster at some point. Her leaving signaled one among the most defining epochs in Bangladesh politics paving way for Dr. Yunus' interim government (Asia-Pacific Research, 2024).

FALL OF SHEIKH HASINA

ECONOMIC AND SOCIAL DISCONTENT

With Sheikh Hasina in power, the economy of the country has been developed rapidly, gross domestic product grew more than by 6 % in the year. This growth was due mainly to the RMG sector where almost 80% of export commodities belong to this sector as indicated in Transparency International 2024. But those economic gains were unequally divided. Farmers and other underprivileged people remained locked in poverty while new unearned wealth poured to elites in urban areas with the backing of economic growth.

The issue was compounded by inflation occurring in the same year that reduce the purchasing capacities of the middle and lower income earners. The average annual inflation rate during Hasina's rule was reported to be around 5-6%, and the food inflation often went beyond especially during emergencies as seen in 2024 update (Al Jazeera). Unemployment, especially among the youth, and especially college educated youth was another persistent problem. Many university leavers find few choices in terms of employment and as a result, young people feel frustrated.

Also, Retail and Miscellaneous goods are economic significant RMG sector was slower because the global environment, competitors such as Vietnam raised, have struck domestic labour issues. They lacked proper working conditions, low wages and no protection for the workers, these factors made them go on frequent strikes and slow productivity (Reuters, 2024). Such pains and other issues alongside the main headlines' allegations of corruption within Hasina's administration were beyond effective political communication to the public. There were informal findings that the government officials embezzled funds, and the latest big failures in corruption undermined confidence in the authorities (Transparency International, 2024).

High inflation, unemployment rate, corruption and high economic disparity produced a social disturbed climate for social unrest. This kind of government was perceived to be a very elitist one and which was out of touch with the common man; this perception became something of a cliché when it came to opposition movements and any civil unrest (Human Rights Watch, 2024).

CHAPTER THREE

THE STUDENT-LED QUOTA MOVEMENT

The quota movement stemmed out of absurdity of perceived discrimination within the civil service recruitment system, however, it has evolved into an increasing displeasure towards Hasina's government. Central to the protests was a proposal that sought to ensure that 56% of government employment opportunities went to the targeted groups of people that included the freedom fighter's dependents, women, people from the ethnic origin and the disabled. Despite the quotas' intention to address deficiencies in the representation of minorities, students pointed out that the quotas generated group interest with as the dominant recruitment factor and in the process harmed the more deserving candidates (The Diplomat, 2024).

It accelerated in weeks of students' national strikes, sit-ins, and marches. To summaries, Dhaka University emerged as the rallying point and participants came from different institutions of learning all over the nation. People took to the streets hoping to force equal representation quotas to be lowered down to 10% and a non-biased recruitment process (Al Jazeera, 2024).

The authorities suppressed these actions since there is no excuse for such protests as people can work through their employers to change the situation. Stones were thrown, tear gas was used, batons and water cannons were used to clear the demonstrators, people were injured, and arrests were made. Footages of tyrannical police assaulting students flooded social media platforms – the people started sympathizing with the protesters. The demonstrations quickly became a critic of governance with sit-in protesters calling for the eradication of corruption, authoritarian rule and especially lack of employment opportunities (The Diplomat, 2024).

This movement was not limited to the demands set by the movement organizers and participants alone. It unveiled bottled up anger of the youths over perceived negligence by the government on issues of inequality and employment. As some critics elaborated, the severe oppression deepened the erosion of legitimacy of Hasina's government and encouraged people to demand her resignation (Human Rights Watch, 2024).

INTERNATIONAL INFLUENCE IN THE REGIME CHANGE

The political transformation inside Bangladesh is largely linked to the external encouragement of the global community towards the Bangladesh political model. Western governments and organisations raised their trend of protesting and human rights abuses as demanding the support of democracy.

Although, according to some analysts, it was geopoliticalsend pointed more to the presence of China in South Asia [Reuters, 2024].

Discipline and impartation of authority was continued to progress under Sheikh Hasina with one more mastery of worsening Bangladesh's economic relation with China through involving the country in Belt and Road Initiative (BRI) projects like Power plants, Highways, and Ports. Such trends became concerning in the capitals of the West, especially of the United States of America, translating China's investment in Bangladesh as part of its moves towards the Indo-Pacific Region expansion (The Diplomat, 2024).

Under this consideration the Nobel laureate Dr. Muhammad Yunus came into picture. Yunus was previously credited for his efforts on microfinance and social businesses, which put him on good stead in the Western world. Their international recognition and especially his support for justice and human rights made him a viable contender against Hasina. As the protests escalated, sources claim that the Western diplomats spoke to Yunus branding him as a potential figure to bring Bangladesh to the democrat western fold (Al Jazeera, 2024).

Western governments, human rights organisations NGOs and the international media complemented each other in focusing on the human rights violations and creeping authoritarianism of Hasina administration. This diplomatic and media pressure made Hasina more lonely in the international level and her position internally became worst. If the pressure increased, along with a decrease in international support, Hasina was forced to resign which allowed Yunus to take charge temporarily (Reuters, 2024).

"BANGLADESH'S POLITICAL TURMOIL: EXAMINING THE QUOTA MOVEMENT AND ITS EFFECTS ON SHEIKH HASINA'S ADMINISTRATION"

The quota movement in Bangladesh has developed from a students demand for change of policy to political crisis involving violence and demand for removal of Prime Minister Sheikh Hasina. This overview will also discuss the background of the movement, consequetics of the scenario especially the BNP and Jamaat-e-Islami's role. Also, it will give background information about Sheikh Hasina's government and her achievement and at the same time arguing other movement.

BACKGROUND OF THE QUOTA MOVEMENT

The quota system of civil service jobs in Bangladesh was first introduced when the government wanted to provide a share of the civil service jobs to the reserved groups. But in recent years, it turned to be debated one due to the opinion that quotas are abused; thus, change is welcomed. It gained support from students specifically targeting CEOs who wanted to eliminate or at least lower the quotas as they considered merit as the best reason to be recruited.

HOW THE QUOTA MOVEMENT STARTED

The appreciation of the quota reform movement started in the year 2018 when the students' formed groups to demonstrate against the existing quota systems arguing that it was a demerit of meritocracy. The demonstrations were taken to the next level following the government move in March 2018 to scrap the less favorable quotas. At first, the students' claims were related to the need to change the quota system only for the benefit of providing equal opportunities for the representatives of the weaker sections of society.

IMPLICATIONS OF THE MOVEMENT

What the men themselves have done to the 'quota movement' is not to be underestimated. Not only has it focused on merit in civil service in Bangladesh, it has also revealed the society's prejudices in representation and discrimination. The protests have brought necessary focus on the fact that merit needs to be combined with social justice to minorities.

CURRENT STATUS

Beginning of July 2024 sees a drastic change in the circumstances whereby; The Appellate Division of the Supreme Court has come up with a ruling for that 7% affirmative action for certain liberate groups such as the freedom fighters and the ethnic groups but opens up 93% for competition. This ruling was considered as the prospective solution to the protests, which still matched the students' demands. However, the movement has a problem of violence with unrests which have more political factions leading to rampage and arson in various regions of the country.

Some open sources state that during July 18-21, intensive fighting took place, and calculated for each of these days the loss in terms of lives of between 30 to 51 people in Dhaka and other cities. There were allegations by medical facilities of the use of live bullets on protesters further demonstrating the regime's willingness to deal with the protests violently. The violence has received global concern, diaspora groups' protests in other nations demanding Hasina's ouster.

POLITICAL HIJACKING OF THE MOVEMENT

The quota movement has been hijacked by the party opposition Bangladesh Nationalist Party (BNP) and Jamaat-e-Islami whose … main agenda are anti-Prime Minister Sheikh Hasina, not the students'. This has led to use of force which includes; fighting, destruction of property and a general degradation of the law and order. Several accounts show that these political groups used students' genuine concerns to advance their causes; thus the non-violent protests end up being a pathway through which political opposition to Hasina's government is waged..

The BNP and Jamaat have been caught in the middle of charges of inciting violence and the protests serve as a tool to overthrow the government. The situation has been so progressed that now armed cadres of these parties have started controlling the protest which often results in the burning of public and private property. The country has been put under a curfew and the military deployed to quell the violence.

Even in Dhaka city, Vandalism and arson attacks have targeted and affected various Government buildings including BTV Center, National Data Center, Bridge Authority Building and many others that include the Disaster Management Authority Building, BRTA Building, Mirpur Indoor Stadium, Building of the Postal Authority, at least two Metro Rail Stations, a number of toll plazas of the Elevated Expressway, BEZA Bhaban, DG Health Office, a number It is important to note that no one and nothing was safe during this unprecendented campaign of violence, not even private properties and transports. There were also testimonies about violence from other parts of Bangladesh, apart from Dhaka. In the specific districts which include Rangpur, Narayanganj, Madaripur and some others, several installations belonging to the Law Enforcement Agencies have been attacked paralyzing several security personnel while leaving several grievously injured and several others having their arms and ammunitions stolen. In one daring attempt, many hundreds of the prisoners, two of whom where Jihadist convicted terrorists, broke out of the district jail of Narshingdi, leading to the theft of the jail's arsenal, and the degradation of the residents' property, quarter of the jail authorities.

SHEIKH HASINA AND HER GOVERNMENT

Bangladesh has witnessed Sheikh Hasina as a key political personality right from the time when she came into power for the first time in 1996. It has been her government that has seen relatively high economic growth, infrastructural development and the overall advancement in social facilities such as education and health. She has also strived in women's rights, poverty and income inequality where her administration has achieved tremendous milestones and she has been recognized internationally.

Nevertheless, the government led by this woman is criticized for suppressing dissent and opposing it. Today's quota movement, however much it had its inception on perfectly valid grounds, has been painted by some as a wrecking ball, designed to bring her government down rather than make constructive changes.

The last disturbances have illuminated the weak points of the government and its illegitimacy, especially as the basic storyline changes from the non-educated population of Yemen to the intellectuals who are now quite actively protesting the actions of the administration

CONCLUSION

The necessary understanding of the interdependence between grass root student movements and political strategies could be observed while analysing the recent quota movement of Bangladesh. In my opinion the earlier part of the demonstrations regarding reform was justifiable, however those following the physical aggression and taking advantage politically have gone too far. In conclusion, the Awami League government under the leadership of Sheikh Hasina has done well in these developments besides managing to address some of these crises when coming to power; however, the new regime is one that must attend to these problems while rebuilding and ensuring students' voice is not hijacked by politically augmented unions. The result of this fighting was expected to redefine the country's politics, economy, as well as its societal structure in the next several years and possibly beyond.

CHAPTER FOUR

DR. MUHAMMAD YUNUS: A PROFILE

PROFESSIONAL ACHIEVEMENTS

Dr. Muhammad Yunus who is widely renowned social entrepreneurs is a Bangladeshi by birth and is born on 28th of June in 1940 in Chittagong. In early 1983, he established Grameen Bank for the poor who want loans up to USD 250 for Micro enterprise without any collateral. This new strategy allowed millions primarily women in rural areas bring out small businesses and become financially empowered (NobelPrize.org, 2006).

The most notable innovation of the Grameen Bank model is that the model has been imitated in more than one hundred countries around the world changing the poverty reduction framework. However, by 2006 Dr. Yunus and Grameen Bank jointly received the Nobel Peace Prize for attempting to establish 'bottom-up' economi and social relief. The Nobel Committee also noted that their demonstration of how the poorest of the poor could be empowered for the purpose of development and or attaining dignity (NobelPrize.org, 2006).

Besides microfinance, Yunus embraced "Social Business" concepts of businesses which not only are financially sustainable but serve the primary aim of solving social issues. He has written several books; the latests of them are Banker to the Poor and Building Social Business: The New Architecture for Microfinance. These contributions have placed him on the spotlight and he has been accorded many awards include the Presidential Medal of Freedom in the United States and the Congressional Gold Medal (DW News, 2023).

CONTROVERSIES AND LEGAL CHALLENGES

Yet, the legal and political persecution of Dr. Yunus has been done, especially in his home country. He faced allegations of embezzlement of donor monies at Grameen Bank in 2011 when he was accused of misappropriating monies. Yunus and his organisations vehemently dismissed these allegations as politically motivated due to tension between his organisations and Sheikh Hasina's government (DW News, 2023).

Relations between Yunus and the Awami League became sour in 2011 when the country's Supreme Court affirmed a ruling that compelled Yunus to relinquish his position as managing director at Grameen Bank. The reason was his old age stated by the court as beyond the retirement age, although a lot of people regarded this as politically motivated and Hasina was said to have regarded Yunus' international profile as a competition to her monopoly (Frontline, 2024).

The following years were turbulent in some other legal problems for Yunus. In January 2024 he was imprisoned for six months together with three officials of Grameen Telecom Company for embezzlement of labor laws. There was also condemned by other human rights group which said that the case was meant to compromise the credibility and impartiality of Yunus. These legal complexes depict the existing strained diplomatic character of Yunus relations with the Bangladeshi political leadership (TIME, 2024).

APPOINTMENT AS INTERIM LEADER

Dr. Yunus was appointed ad interim chief advisor in 2024 during severe political crises in Bangladesh. Amid opposition protests and student demands for political change, Yunus emerged as a compromise candidate to guide the nation through transition. His non-partisan and upright reputation gained international recognition, bolstering his campaign (Reuters, 2024).

Western governments and NGOs placed themselves on the side of Yunus demanding that he installed to lead the Bangladesh as an interim leader. It is for this particular reason that he politically aligned with values of democracy and human rights making him a preferable candidate to other international actors who are battling it out with China in the region

Yunus himself was quite clear about presenting his leadership as the way to return Bangladesh to the path of democracy and rebuild the severed ties with the West (The Wall Street Journal, 2024).

However, his appointment had not been without controversy before even being enacted. His opponents stated that Yunus had no prior experience of governance and others opined that the disease would be worse than the cure, or in other words, his leadership might increase the division of the society instead of minimizing it. Others say that he relied heavily on foreign interventions, sovereignty and domestic politics management issues were of concern (The Wall Street Journal, 2024).

CHALLENGES OF FIRST 100 DAYS

GOVERNANCE CHANGES

It has been a turbulent first 100 days for Bangladesh's interim Dr. Yunus government: widespread lawlessness, rising Islamist militancy, and a declining authority of governance structures. With an increasing extrajudicial killings, forced disappearances, and targeted violence, institutional accountability has collapsed. This instability has most heavily impacted minority communities such as Hindus, Buddhists and Christians. During the Durga Puja (festival time of the Hindu goddess Durga), the desecration of Hindu idols and the violent intimidation of minorities reveal deepening security debacle and weak government's record to protect vulnerable groups (Human Rights Watch, 2024; The Daily Star, 2024).

Hasina's ouster created political vacuum that Islamist militants have exploited to gain unprecedented influence in governance and in society. When there is no opposition, these groups have done away with secular organizations and promoted radical rhetoric. The government's neglect has thrown open the door for Islamists to secure a grip on Bangladeshi politics, undermining secular and pluralistic roots of the country. National stability and regional security as a whole are undermined; unchecked radicalization poses cross border implications (AP News, 2024).

Under the Yunus administration civil liberties have eroded further. Political pressure has been increasingly retransmitted into silencing systematic opposition, and restrictions on civil society organizations have reached an unprecedented level, such as the stifling of dissent and the independent advocacy. Sophisticated exclusionary and authoritarian approach to governance has exacerbated polarization of the society, fuelled mistrust and hostility. Without fast corrective measures to bring back accountability, inclusivity and democratic norms, which Bangladesh, unless substantial efforts are made, is destined to pass a dangerous phase that would escalate into prolonged instability and jeopardise both socio political and economic future as much as the Diplomat (2024) has prophesied.

ECONOMIC CHALLENGES

The political economy of the country when Yunus started his first one hundred days was not propitious. Average inflation cheered to the rate of 13% in September 2024 especially due to increase in price of food and energy. This rising inflation especially affected the middle and lower incomes adversely, the erosion of the purchasing power caused further declining satisfaction among the public (Reuters, 2024). In order to avert this crisis, the central bank has sought to increase its key interest rate to 10 percent, as a means of bringing down the prices. Although this measure made costs higher and utility lower, it spiked the borrowing costs, which was another leverage for the small businesses and entrepreneurs (Financial Times, 2024).

The garment industry which is the major export earning sector of Bangladesh dealing 80% of the export income of the country suffered a lot. They felt they could not rely on the imported material due to political instability, which meant that they placed fewer orders thus having a beggarly effect on production. Protests and demonstrations in this important province also affected other such sectors as labour strikes and disputes pushed the livelihoods of millions of workers relying in this sector in jeopardy (The Diplomat, 2024).

The initiation of IMF fund and other international organization's financial aid was ill received by the government. The government required $5bn for supporting its economy and foreign exchange reserves dearth but high-level concerns of governance coupled issue of policy inconsistency made seeking help difficult (Reuters, 2024). Several critics also criticized that Yunus had been more concerned with following the dictates of his international donors more than the Grameen economic policies were responding to the rural poor clients he had advocated for during his stay at the Grameen Bank (Human Rights Watch, 2024).

SOCIAL INSTABILITY AND VIOLENCE

Social tensions were elevated to dangerous levels during Yunus initial period of leadership. Sectarianism increases and is a volatile factor that brought more conflicts and minority people, in particular, Hindus, Buddhists, Christian were being target. In its report for October 2024, several cases were also noted of Hindu community members being attacked or threatened during Durga Puja which made people feel insecure and insecure about the security situation of Bangladeshi minorities (Dhaka Tribune 2024).

The authorities failed to control the rioting; according to various sources, more than thirty thousand people, including 3,500 policemen, were killed in violence during this period. People attributed the break of law and order by the government and human rights watch organizations recorded forced evictions, rape among other violation of human rights (Human Rights Watch, 2024).

This prompted a rise of hardline Islamist within the government, which only added to existing concern of radicalization. Critics said that Yunus' administration indirectly strengthened the position of fundamentalist groups that take advantage of the fact that the authorities weakened moderate opponents (The Daily Star, 2024).

REPRESSION OF HASINA'S SUPPORTERS

In this interim government committed some steps against the supporters of Sheikh Hasina and her Awami League Dr Yunus. Main accused and other leaders of the Awami League were arrested in corruption and dictatorship charges during their rule. People said that these arrest were looking only politically motivated and hence were made to establish the supremacy of Yunus when it comes to tackling issues of corruption (The Diplomat, 2024).

Pro Hasina media stations were throttled and threatened. Some newspapers were said to have been closed and some journalists arrested, radio and television broadcasts were restricted from covering activities deemed unfavorable to the interim government. Such actions provoked criticism from international associations of human rights and were classified as a violation of media freedom (Reuters, 2024).

While using such actions as the government tried to argue that such actions were necessary to bring back order into the society, such moves only exacerbated existing divisions across the country. The political opponents criticized Yunus for being authoritarian and sought to deny him the support that a leader who supports pluralism deserves (Dhaka Tribune, 2024).

INTERNATIONAL AND DOMESTIC REACTIONS

GLOBAL CRITICISM

The international community observed as a political and social transformations intensifying in the territory under the interim government of Dr. Yunus. For the initial few years after the events of September 11, 2001, Yunus was seen by many western countries as the face of the democratic change as he had received the Nobel Peace Prize and wen advocating for social justice worldwide. However, when combined fresh trends in human rights violations and rising levels of political oppression became apparent the trend changed.

America's key strategic partner, India, was one of the first countries to strongly oppose Yunus' policies. As the violent attacks on Indian students in Bangladesh occurred, coupled with an escalation of sectarian violence that targeted Hindus, Buddhists and Christians, the relation between India and Bangladesh was worst affected. New Delhi was particularly worried by assault on Hindus – most of whom may be related culturally or through consanguinity with people in India (The Diplomat, 2024). This was aggravated by increasing dependence on Islamist factions by Yunis which India thought could increase extremism and destabilize the region (Al jazeera, 2024).

Initially, the western governments also exhibited similar enthusiasm as the Nobel committee in putting their trust and faith in Yunus as the leader of a developing country's economy. Claims of media suppression, political detentions and violence against political dissidents also brought negative Image building into perspective for Yunus. There are human rights organisations such as amnesty International and Human Rights Watch raised concerns of forced disappearances and extrajudicial killings of the first 100 days in office. Amnesty International regards the situation in Bangladesh as a grave human rights issue, and Human Rights Watch urged launching an inquiry into the reports of abuses committed by the Army under the leadership of Yunus (Amnesty International, 2024; Human Rights Watch, 2024).

These criticisms also applied to the international legal domains. Litigations were initiated in different foreign jurisdictions against Yunus' government for several acts of gross violation of human rights including the forceful expulsion of the religious groups from their ancestral homes besides the acts of politics repression. That development pointed to increased isolation of Bangladesh internationally as the future unfolded. UNHRC also called statements fearing the newly emerged interim government to adopt democratic tenets and protect the rights of minorities (UNHRC, 2024).

Yunus tried to safeguard the Western patronage by insisting on the government's good intentions for the economic reforms and fight against corruption. He justified his actions as rightful to dismantle an unstable political and economically vulnerable country. However, little was spun through this narrative as more independence media houses and International Non-governmental organizations reported an escalation of the repression under his administration (The Guardian, 2024).

LOCAL OPPOSITION AND CONTINUED PROTESTS

At home, Yunus faced a challenging political environment for his operations and activities. Growing dissatisfaction led various groups to seek the removal of him and his interim government. People's organizations, students, and anti-military factions of the Awami League began street protests advocating for free elections and democratic practices throughout the nation. These organizations are attempting to hold peaceful protests; however, the Army and other government forces are being used to disband them, which has contributed to the country's challenges.

Political activists who were active in the student movement that helped remove the Prime Minister Sheikh Hasina were among the harshest critics of Yunus. Many people were disappointed by the government which he headed over the lack of attempts to solve general problems like unemployment, corruption, and inflation rates. Violent actions in protesting continued to escalate especially on the university campuses where student rose against Police force. Policing involved tear gas and water cannons making several students to get injured while its brutal crackdown also resulted into mass condemnations of the government (Dhaka Tribune, 2024).

The Awami League became weakened after Hasina's departure but nonetheless was able to organize and use the population's frustration with Yunus against him. Its leaders complained the interim government was arresting political opponents under the pretext of fighting graft. A wave of active political repression in the form of publicized raids against the Awami League members and activists was viewed by many people as the party's deliberate attempt to weaken the organization. These actions further inspired party supporters to be part of the increasing number of protests aiming at a free election and restoration of political liberty (The Daily Star, 2024).

Forces of civil society and minorities religious also complained of rising sectarian violence and the lack of responsibility by the government in protecting the vulnerable groups. Some of the alleged attacks were reported to have taken place during Hindu religious festivals other alleged attacks included destruction of properties owned by the minority that triggered aggressive sentiments when combined with perceptions of a systematic process of elimination under Yunus regime. These acts were publicized by advocacy groups during international forums to press for protection of minority rights (Amnesty International, 2024).

Other issues with regards to economy added to the fury of the people. Things like inflation, break down in exports and massive layoffs in key sectors such as garment factories made economic difficulties became the order of the day. Industrial workers and other groups affiliated with labour unions and trade organizations were part of the demonstrators insisting on ways to restore the economy and ensure decent job representation to employees. More strikes at factories concentrating in the garment industry that constitute a major part of Bangladesh's GDP made its stability even worse (Financial Times, 2024).

The political instability in Bangladesh at the time created a challenging environment for Yunus's administration.   Several attempts by his administration to implement changes suggested by critics were viewed as inadequate or delayed. Additionally, corporate elitism influenced the reform process, contributing to public distrust and isolating Yunus in managing both domestic and international affairs (The Guardian, 2024).

CHAPTER FIVE

IMPLICATIONS FOR BANGLADESH'S FUTURE

GOVERNANCE AND STABILITY RISKS

The signs of the present political climate for the Yunus administration in Bangladesh is causing much anxiety in the prospects of democracy and governance in Bangladesh. The principal political players, including the Awami league, excluded from the political process deliberately, have generated high political radicalization in Bangladesh. This exclusion together with exclusion of the minority in the governance model has ensured that the governance model caters more to this certain groups of the society rather than the whole society. This support of the administration for seemingly Islamic parties pushes the secular and liberals to the side while deepening the cleavages in society and increasing the volatility of radical politics (Human Rights Watch, 2024).

The said trends are a significant threat to democracy and may well accelerate the slide into authoritarianism.
Democracy is systematically being rolled back, and despite the lack of these tools, it is becoming

infinitely more challenging to put through real change. Concerns have been raised that this curve could extended social destabilisation, stunted economic growth and increased security volatility in this time frame (Asia Society, 2024). If Bangladeshi political elites continue to fail to advance inclusive governance, and reclaim democratic tradition, then the later political stability of Bangladesh would be uncertain. It is high time the international community acted to find sustainable solutions and politically transform states to uphold democracy or guarantee individual rights to minorities.

ECONOMIC CONSEQUENCES

Dr. Muhammad Yunus', interim government, has also promulgated its own economic reforms, notably the encouragement of Sharia based Financial systems, while enduring the negative consequences of prevailing political violence. Push for Islamic finance is one of the most significant policy shifts and in this regard, we have seen the creation of a specialty Islamic capital market on the Dhaka Stock Exchange. The intent is in line with global trends of Sharia compliant investment, which will attract funds committed to Islamic principles of excluding interest based transactions. But, such changes have worried secular Economists and Financial experts that these changes will be inclusive practice at the cost of marginalisation of conventional Banking system (Bangladesh Think Tank Forum, 2024).

At the same time, the political violence plaguing the administration's early term has raged quite on the country's economy. During the period July-October

2024, at least 389 members of the Awami League and its affiliates were killed, with many of those attacks intentionally targeting the destruction of businesses, properties, and neighbourhood infrastructure. This violence disrupts economic activity in the regions it hits, but this has reduced productivity and frightened off both domestic and foreign investments. Furthermore, there is uncertainty regarding such evidence tampering, media censorship and general undermining of public trust in governance and economic institutions (Primary Death List of ALBD, 2024).

And symbolic and structural disruptions have compounded it with the erosion of public trust. The destruction of some 1,500 sculptures, murals and memorials across the country and interference in education and civic services underline the economic problems facing the Yunus government. Readers often impute these attempts to the legacy of rising Islamist influence, designed to undermine the country's secular nature and intensify economic as well as social instability (Bangladesh Think Tank Forum, 2024).

While the promise of Sharia based financial reforms has been made, the government has failed to tackle the wider economic impact that such disruptions could have. Behind any potential economic gains have loomed delays in infrastructure projects, as well as concerns about the power of Islamist factions. If the administration cannot ensure public safety and political stability they risk undermining its broader economic ambitions and putting the country at a pivotal point where there is need for effective policymaking.

REGIONAL AND GLOBAL DYNAMICS

Bangladesh's regional relations have also been tested during Yunus's tenure of interim leadership. Another major regional power is India which became worried about the increase of anti-India propaganda and more frequent assaults on India-related minorities, such as Hindus – who are culturally and closer related to Indians. These new developments New Delhi perceives as problematic for Bangladesh's stability and stability of the entire South Asian region (Asia Society, 2024).

At the same time, Bangladesh's increasing dependence on China as an investment source produces fresh geography. Bangladeshi government through Belt & Road Initiative (BRI) projects have increased Beijing's economic influence in Bangladesh, majorly by investing in infrastructural and energy sectors. This is helpful economically but at the same time poses implementing problems on behalf of Dhaka currently being overly reliant on China thus greatly endangering its foreign policy autonomy (Asia Society, 2024).

These dynamics carry geopolitical overtones for South Asian region's. The geographical characteristics of Bangladesh being in the centre of the strategic competition between the USA and China can influence it through Yunus's foreign policy actions. Concerning the dilemma between depending more on China or the western nation, scholars observe that relying with the either part will isolate important regional partners and deepen the complexity of BM's foreign policies (Carnegie Endowment, 2024).

The challenges of managing a transitional period in governance have been put as the first 100 days of Dr. Yunus's interim government show. Though the government in various countries of the world has endeavored to stabilize the nations through introduced reforms, its tact on suppressing dissent, and challenging failure to address economic and social grievances have been severely criticized. These development have implications that are not only political and concern the future of democracy in Bangladesh but also economic and concern the path that Bangladesh's economy takes in the near future and the nature of its relations with its neighbors. The coming months are therefore crucial in establishing if Yunus is capable of leading the county's effort to overcome these challenges or compound them.

RECOMMENDATIONS

RESTORING GOVERNANCE AND RULE OF LAW

Immediate Elections and Inclusive Governance
At the very top, it should be the firm position of the interim government of Dr. Yunus that the first

priority is to hold free and fair elections without delay. Obviously if electoral process should be restored and restore public trust and democratic legitimacy, all the political parties should be included including the Awami League. To avoid bias or manipulation accusations of which to be held accountable as the caretaker government, the elections should be overseen by a neutral caretaker government (Bangladesh Think Tank Forum, 2024). Cease Structural Reforms under Current Leadership Thus, Dr. Yunus must suspend all the structural changes that have not received support of a representative government or the wider populace. Instead, these changes should be shifted to a democratically elected administration, made inclusive and sustainable.

REINSTATE SECULAR GOVERNANCE PRINCIPLES

Action needs to be taken immediately to reduce the growing power of Islamist militants. But if the radical groups are allowed to function and minority communities are not protected, then the government must reaffirm Bangladesh's secular commitment. It means prosecuting perpetrators of hate crimes, and securing justice for victims of sectarian violence (Human Rights Watch, 2024).

REBUILD TRUST WITH CIVIL SOCIETY AND MINORITIES

In the meantime, the interim administration should hold dialogue with civil societies organisations, religious minorities and marginalised groups to reconcile unity and to address grievances. By laying a foundation for reconciliation, platforms establishing where these stakeholders can participate in governance can help reduce polarization (The Diplomat, 2024).

ECONOMIC RECOVERY STRATEGIES

Economic development is extremely crucial to political stability and therefore it is necessary for Bangladesh to solve several very important problems to achieve economic growth. Among them one of the major agendas is the need to renew the garment industry which contributes 80% of Bangladesh' export revenues. The government needs to adopt policies that would encourage the international buyers to return to sourcing from Bangladesh through the following ways; By fixing labor rights, addressing political instability and upgrading working conditions (The Daily Star, 2024). It also remains possible to support investment in this important segment through the provision of tax incentives and subsidies for garment manufacturers (International Finance, 2024).

Another important issue is regulating inflation rates. The government is to minimize cases of inflation in the country. Thus, the annual inflation rate raised to 13% in September 2024, food prices were rising especially putting great pressure on the poor. In the light of this, policies that spur production of food crops for local consumption as well as diminish lobbying for imported products need to be given much attention. Outlays on local agriculture and support toward necessary products might support IMR needs to the precariously now (International Finance, 2024).

Bangladesh should also try to obtain its funds from multilateral organizations such as the International Monetary Fund (IMF), the World Bank etc. States should provide credits to finance welfare projects and combat poverty in order to secure the economy and address the problem of inequality. Whereas, such financial relations must be complemented the governance improvements to ensure international counterparts that the government is also devoted to accountability and transparency (The World Bank, 2024).

Building up the image of Bangladesh also plays a significant role in this circumstance of FDI inflow. Human rights issues that were voiced during the first one hundred days of Yunus' administration can restore international confidence. Dr. Yunus with a Nobel laureate behind him could be instrumental in entering into new trade relations and new business deals with western countries (The World Bank, 2024).

INTERNATIONAL MEDIATION FOR DEMOCRATIC TRANSITION

Thus, Bangladesh is likely to come back to democracy by next year's election but only with the active involvement of world and regional actors. As previously stated the United Nations as well as the South Asian Association for Regional Cooperation (SAARC) are capable enough and can help political parties come into negotiations. It can incorporate all the stakeholders into the transition process, and values democracy (Bangladesh Rural Council, 2021).

South Asian players particularly India and China have to ensure stability in Bangladesh as well. Delhi believed the problems such as increase in anti-Indian stance, and apparant offences against the minorities in India could be addresses through diplomacy. So also, it is with respect to China's increasing heft through investments across Bangladesh's infrastructure: the more the latter comes under China's possession, the more it must be also shielded from China's control over Bangladesh's foreign policymaking and state sovereignty (Asia Society, 2024).

The USA and the EU, as well as other Western countries that support the Bangladesh government, should link their investments in the Bangladesh economy and their trade relations to the improvement of the situation with the democratization of the country's political system and the protection of human rights. These conditions may encourage the transitional government towards getting closer to international norms and values to adopt democratic transitions (Carnegie Endowment, 2024).

CONCLUSION

SUMMARY OF KEY DEVELOPMENTS

Interim government is not a term typically associated with stability, and the first 100 days of Dr. Muhammad Yunus' administration have been marked by significant political changes. He came to power by replacing Sheikh Hasina, which was viewed by some as an opportunity to address the grievances of the oppression and other political and structural issues. However, his administration has faced increasing criticism regarding governance, economic management, and alleged authoritarianism.

Since the accession of Yunus to power, governance reforms have been geared towards dismantling structures of the preceding regime hence shedding a political aspect on most of the actions carried out. The action to dissolve the Bangladesh Chhatra League and the arrest of key leaders of the Awami League were perceived as efforts to sap power than making room for apprenticeship. New constitutional changes that limit even more the activities of the opposition have worried the civil society and the international community regarding the democratic decline (Human Rights Watch, 2024).

From the economical perspective, the interim government has been very problematic. This led to an increase in inflation rates to the highest level touching the lives of the mid and low affects earners most. It is a verified information that garment industry is one of the most important sectors of Bangladeshi economy which already faced a decline in exports because of political crisis and strikes. These economic problems together with questions from other countries about the quality of governance have affected FDI and diplomatic relations with major partners (The World Bank, 2024).

The decade has also witnessed an increased level of extra judicial killings and sectarian violence in Bangladesh. These include; Adding to this, the religious minorities have recently been attacked, many innocent people have been forced to displaced and violence against women is also on the rise, all these making it clear that law and order situation is worsening. These problems not only intensified internal division but also harm Bangladesh's image internationally (Human Rights Watch, 2024).

This report has also examined several factors contributing to Sheikh Hasina's challenges, including public dissatisfaction, student demands for quota reforms, and interference by foreign organizations. Upon assuming office, Hasina was well into her fourth term and had become adept at both fostering growth and navigating political turbulence. She undoubtedly prepared the political landscape for significant changes, addressing the country's economic conditions. Nonetheless, Dr. Yunus inherited a highly polarized political and economic system characterized by economic stagnation and weak institutions, presenting numerous challenges.

Dr. Yunus' administration inherited the challenging task of addressing societal needs amidst continuous and volatile economic shocks while also implementing structural changes to foster a stable socioeconomic environment. However, its governance structures, exclusionary practices, and coercive behaviors have cast doubt on the interim government's viability. The social unrest and economic uncertainty observed in the first one hundred days suggest that without significant changes in current trends, both the political and economic development of Bangladesh remain uncertain.

CALL FOR UNITY AND DEMOCRATIC RESTORATION

Bangladesh is currently at a critical juncture. The decisions made during this period will shape the historical perspective of Dr. Yunus's interim government and determine the future direction of the nation. Commitment to these decisions is essential, as it will influence the public's perception and support for the pursuit, restoration, and maintenance of democratic governance and socio-economic equity.

One of the significant issues is the need for initiatives focused on promoting national unity as a core value. Political polarization between parties, along with the oversight of key stakeholders, has contributed to a fragmented political landscape in Bangladesh. It is recommended that Dr. Yunus' administration engage individuals from diverse political backgrounds, including members of the opposition, civil society organizations, opposition leaders in student unions, and minority groups to collaboratively determine the nation's path forward. This dialogue may help restore public trust in authorities and reduce political confrontations (The Diplomat, 2024).

The reestablishment of democracy and free-market institutions is essential. Democracy must be reconstructed, including the restoration of the caretaker government system, which has historically played a crucial role in ensuring free and fair elections. International observers can assist in this process and ensure neutrality in upcoming elections. Additionally, protecting the rule of law necessitates defending judicial independence, preventing the legal system from being used as a political tool (Asia Society, 2024).

The TWNW has important role of supporting Bangladesh during this transition period and make Bangladesh Asian tiger. Moreover, using economic motivation in the form of trade or international financial sources, and political pressure, the interim government can be encouraged to adopt liberal democratization and human rights to people. As for the India- Bangladesh relationship, other regional players like India or China also have a stake in Bangladesh's stability and elaboration, they have to play the positive role in and improve the bilateral relation (Carnegie Endowment, 2024).

Still more the social and sectarian violence is of equal significance. Recent changes in the types of attacks, which are increasingly aimed at religious minorities and other persecuted communities, answer the question on consistent development of changes in law enforcement structures. The public can be assured through successful execution of programs aimed at involving the security forces towards human rights and community training. Further, hate speech and propaganda threatening divisions within society remain imminent and should be relentlessly fought by the government (Human Rights Watch, 2024).

Finally, it is important for Dr. Yunus to understand the sentiments of the people of Bangladesh if he wishes to maintain his legacy from the Nobel Peace Prize. Policies that divide are no longer acceptable. Religious minorities should be protected, and political and press freedom should be upheld. Additionally, efforts should be made to curb the rise of militant groups to prevent instability in the country.

Although the above challenges are evident in Dr. Yunus' administration it is capable of uplifting Bangladesh in to a better position if it addresses these challenges. As a Nobel laureate Yunus can attract global partners to back up his development vision of a democratic Bangladeshi society. But this will have to be built with an understanding that the institutions of civil society will expect openness, responsibility and good governance.

The situation presented above and the challenges described all apply to the first one hundred days of work of the interim government of Dr. Yunus in Bangladesh. Elected to power with the hope that the nation's new leader will bring change to the nation

and its citizen, the times of governance,
management of the economy, and social order has
brought it to the test of leadership. The fluctuation
which characterized this period is an indication of
the challenges that transitional leadership entails in
a divided country.

CHAPTER SIX

UNDER DR. YUNUS, BANGLADESH IS ESSENTIALLY BECOMING A SAFE HAVEN FOR ISLAMIST MILITANTS

AN INTRODUCTION

Bangladesh has undergone significant changes in its social and political landscape over the past two years. Following a recent student-led movement that resulted in the fall of Sheikh Hasina's government, the country has become increasingly unstable. Nobel laureate Dr. Yunus is now leading the nation under an interim government. Bangladesh is perceived as compromising secular principles by granting immunity to Jamat-e-Islami and Hizbat Tahrir, far-right militant groups. Global security concerns have heightened under Dr. Yunus's administration. This article reviews the ineffective policies implemented by the nascent government and the rise in radicalism and lawlessness. It draws on several notable news articles to analyze the current chaotic and unlawful societal conditions in Bangladesh.

DR YUNUS COHESIVE AND IMPUNITY POLICY TOWARDS RADICAL GROUPS

Dr Yunus has widely been known as a figured and seasoned global icon of Bangladesh. However, the recent turmoil in Bangladesh proved him to be antithetical to core values of peace and security. His leniency towards notorious and than prescribed organisations raised concerns for Bangladesh generally and international community particularly. Radical organisations like Jamat-e-Islami and Hizbat Tahrir possess notorious history in destabilizing the country. Moreover, Dr Yunus government has lifted the ban on Jamat-e-Islami and has released its leaders those were arrested on grave a charges. These tacit support for these organisations of contemporary government has threatened the underlying principles of Bangladesh.

CONTAINMENT OF RADICAL GROUPS UNDER HASINA'S GOVERNMENT.

Sheikh Hasina's Government has discouraged these radical groups and taken an aggressive charge against militancy. However, the radical ideologies were strictly discouraged by previous government. During 15 years tenure of previous government these has crushed by Sheikh Hasina administration. Certain intelligence based operations (IBOs) were conducted with help of intelligence networks and direct military interventions. Leaders of far right group Jamat-e-Islami were trialed and put justice by swift hearings.

Under Hasina Wajid administration these faction has marginalized by law enforcement agencies and were deemed as direct threat to Nation's security. Being as hardliner against these militant groups, than government has often been termed as authoritarian government. As a contrast Dr. Yunus encourage Jamat-e-Islami publically and referred it as an allied party. Jamat-e-Islami prisoners has been released and all cases against these individuals has been removed. Dr. Yunus termed marginalization of Jamat-e-Islami as a politically motivated crackdown by Sheikh Hasina regime past decade.

ECONOMIC STABILITY UNDER HASINA: BALANCING HARDSHIPS AND SECURITY

The economic boom during Sheikh Hasina Government often exemplified by other nations in the region. Economic wellbeing of the Bangladesh society was exceptional despite of struggle and resource -depleted nation. Progress of Bangladesh economy and diminishing poverty number hindered risk of marginalisation of people. During 2022 Bangladesh GDP was recorded as having fastest growth upto 7.2 percent (Al Jazeera , 2024).

This historic economic progress of Bangladesh has made it leader in textile exporting countries. On the other hand, Dr Yunus Government has drastically impacted the economic growth and growing chaos has led this nation to economic uncertainty. On the other hand, economy has been widely impacted under Dr. Yunus regime. It has been reported that more than 100 garments factories has been shut down which make economic progress of Bangladesh even worse (Chaudhury, 2024).

THE PROGRESS OF WOMEN AND LGBTQ COMMUNITIES UNDER SHEIKH HASINA

Sheikh Hasina's government although was not based purely on secular principles. However, women rights were greatly safeguarded during 15 year rule. Specifically, encouraging of inclusivity has practiced by government and women has given equal employment, educational and political participations. Moreover, these step has led to building of progressive environment. Besides, Dr Yunus regime has proved it antithetical to secular and inclusive principles. As, Dr Yunus government has been backed by far right religious militant groups, therefore extremist ideologies discourage LGBTQ right activists and deem them as threat to Bangladeshi society. Between August 5th and Aug 24th this year, 4 cases of rape and torture against women. Moreover, 953 cases of vandalisation and looting has been reported across 8 divisions of Bangladesh.

CHAOS AND INSECURITY UNDER DR. YUNUS GOVERNMENT

Dr. Yunus regime has widely hindered the lawfulness in society and Les to chaotic social environment. It has been identified that security and peacefulness greatly threatened since this chaotic phase of this South Asian nation begin in July, 2024. This prevailing sense of insecurity has widely been administered in educational institutions where government backed far right student organizations has been staging rallies and protests. These extremist backed protests and rallies deter government to compromise basic democratic rights of the socket. Violence has become prevalent in Bangladesh since inception of Dr. Yunus government. 915 cases of house burnings and lootings has been reported across major cities of Bangladesh. As Bangladesh was purely based on secular-democratic principle, Dr Yunus now leading it to become Muslim-Democratic nation.

BANGLADESH DESCENDING INTO LAWLESSNESS AND THE AFGHAN PARALLEL

Progressive radicalization of Bangladesh has posed imminent threats of it becoming as an Afghan parallel in Southern Asia. Moreover, the diminishing lawfulness and uplifting of extremist ideologies has threatened the global peace immensely. In addition, proliferation of anti-secular and democratic ideas could lead to similar political and social Chao as of Afghanistan. As a far right group was banned by previous government back in 2013 due to its links with Pakistan forces during independence.

Further, Dr Yunus government has lifted the ban on proscribed organization "Jamat-i-Islami" and gave opportunity to participate in mainstream politics (Al Jazeera, 2024). Encouraging these groups has greatly threatened peace and risk of proliferating extremist ideologies and principles. The youth of Bangladesh has been drastically radicalised due to recent upsurge of government supported extremist groups. Staging of daily protests has become a new routine in Bangladesh, during recent protest by Hizbat Tahrir students staged the protest bearing ISIS banners (Sharma, 2024). These instances has proved that Bangladeshi society heading towards utter lawlessness and could lead to complete takeover of government by extremist groups.

SECURITY IMPLICATIONS FOR GLOBAL PEACE

Security implications has become evident due to contemporary development in Bangladesh under Dr. Yunus regime. The autocratic government has threatened global community and South Asia at large. In addition, media houses has been kept under immense threat against reporting and criticising current government, these instances has led to growing need of intervention by global society. Moreover, the rise of Islamic militancy threatened the strategic location of the country.

Geographically, Bangladesh located in the region where extremism has been experiencing a surge in past three Decades. Likewise, Pakistan and Afghanistan, the taking over of Bangladesh by pro extremist Dr. Yunus regime would prove vulnerable to the global peace and prosperity. In addition, the diminishing economy and unemployment could lead to refugee crisis to the neighboring countries. India could be directly impacted by this influx of migrants. Therefore, global community must step forward to thwart this growing threat of destabilizing South Asian region.

LAWLESSNESS, INTOLERANCE AND RADICALISED SOCIETY

Violence has been identified as prevalent in Bangladesh since toppling of Sheikh Hasina government. Rising cases of lawlessness like homicides, enforced disappearances and rapes has been reported. Exploitation and extortion of political dissidents and ideological opponents has been on rise under Dr. Yunus regime. Women has been fell victim to the conservative and radical ideologies of far right religious groups. Religious insecurity and intolerance has become prevalent factor in Bangladesh, incidents of vandalisation against religious placed increased drastically. It has been reported that 69 cases of such instances has been orchestrated in the month of August this year. In addition, the articles that has revered as sacred in Hinduism has also been stolen from Jeshoreshwari temple in Shyamnagar (ANI, 2024). These instances are abrupt warning of intense religious intolerance and proliferation of radical ideologies in Bangladeshi society.

CONCLUSION

To conclude this it could be held that the South Asian nation heading towards ultimate chaos, intolerance, destabilization. Moreover, Under Dr. Yunus regime harboring of radical and far right extremist groups has led to threatening of basic principles of the country. The growing militancy has impacted lawfulness and threatened regional security specifically and global peace generally. The measure that had adopt by Sheikh Hasina against extremism and radicalization has now been greatly affected. Scores of lawlessness incidents has been reported across Bangladesh during contemporary regime. Dr. Yunus regime has orchestrated extreme intolerance to political dissidents which led to scores of enforced disappearances by law enforcement agencies. The growing uncertainty in Bangladesh must be stopped at urgent basis and global community should step forward in curibing extremism and unlawfulness in Bangladeshi society.

CHAPTER SEVEN

"BANGLADESH IS ON THE VERGE OF BECOMING AFGHANISTAN 2.0"

INTRODUCTION

Bangladesh, known for its resilience and dynamic culture, has changed dramatically since 1971. Bangladesh has historically suffered from natural calamities, economic problems, and political upheaval. Bangladesh has one of the world's fastest-growing economies due to its textile industry, remittances from abroad workers, and fast-growing technology sector. But new developments have made some wonder what the future holds for the country. Bangladeshis fear that their country is transforming into "Afghanistan 2.0" due to political instability, Islamist terrorist organizations, and the potential loss of human liberties.

RECENT ECONOMIC GROWTH

The textile sector has created millions of employment, reduced poverty, and increased exports. It has been noted that textile industry has become the leading industry to employee thousands of Bangladeshis. Healthcare and education have raised national standards of life. But recent political upheaval resulted in corruption, social discontent, and political instability and casted doubt on the in viability of this economic struggle. Textile industry has been very important for the GDP growth of the country, therefore any upheaval in the political sphere of the country would dent the economic progress. Textile industry has been very important for the GDP growth of the country, The Foreign Investors' Chamber of Commerce and Industry (Ficci) expects even harsher fines after the shutdown significantly impacted Bangladesh's economy with over $10 billion and fast-moving consumer products sector lost over $100 million (Akriti, 2024). Besides, more than 170 clothing manufacturers have gone out of business due to anarchy and a lack of order. The average Bangladeshi confronts a number of difficulties as a result of the political and social unrest in the nation, including inflation, rising prices for basic necessities, and shortages of vital services like power.

EFFECTS OF HASINA'S OUSTER

Effects of Hasina's Ouster has fueled political tensions in Bangladesh have increased since Prime Minister Sheikh Hasina's departure. Opposition parties have slammed her autocratic administration. Her disappearance created a political vacuum where many factions compete for power. This instability has worsened the country's economy, causing investors to lose faith and impeding progress. Political conflicts and social discontent threaten economic growth. Political victimization has abruptly increase after August 5th, and Cyber

Security Act 2023 has strictly been used as a tool to suppress the freedom of speech of political dissidents (TBS Report, 2024).

RISE OF MILITANT ISLAMIST GROUPS

Extremist in Bangladesh has worsen and Bangladeshi extreme Islamist groups have triumphed amid political upheaval. Jamaat-e-Islami and Hefazat-e-Islam secretly promote conservative Islam. These organizations used the government's weakness to recruit new members and advance their ideas. These parties are undermining Bangladesh's secularism and War of Independence beliefs. Moreover, Chief Advisor Dr Muhammad Yunus has lifted the ban on Jamat-e-Islami which makes it clear that contemporary government in Bangladesh heading it to a radical state (Al Jazeera, 2024).

INVIABLE GROUPS BREAKS DORMANCY

Many formerly dormant militant groups are reemerging, bolstered by political instability. Their comeback is more than just ideological bluster; they are actively working to influence Bangladesh's societal norms. The interim administration, lacking the authority and control required to successfully battle these organizations, has unintentionally supplied them with a sense of impunity. Violent extremism and strict interpretations of Sharia law pose an increasingly grave danger to society as they gain momentum, leading to significant social disruptions.

VIOLATION OF WOMEN RIGHTS

The potential erosion of women's rights is one of the most worrisome elements of this upsurge in militant activity. Reportedly, women would soon be required to conform to retrograde standards reminiscent of those enforced by the Taliban in Afghanistan, when they encountered considerable restrictions on their independence and liberties. Implementation of Islamic Law has been regarded as eminent. Sharia law's possible implementation in Bangladesh is moving from the realm of faraway horror to that of imminent reality. Historically, women in Bangladesh have achieved progress in a variety of fields, including education and work. However, as Islamist organizations gain control, there is rising concern that women would be restricted to conventional roles and denied their rights and freedoms.

ENFORCEMENT OF SHARIA CODE

As extremist groups solidify their influence, they become more open about their desire to apply Sharia rules throughout the nation. This action would have disastrous consequences for the secular legal system established after independence, endangering the rights of minorities, women, and everyone who disagrees with their ideas. The societal fabric, stitched with threads of tolerance and variety, is at risk of unravelling.

STUDENTS INHERENT POLITICS AND EXTREMISM

According to recent allegations, many of the student leaders who organized the student quota movement are members of the Bangladeshi extremist party Jamaat-e-Islami. Out of around 150 student leaders, 120 are part of this group. The alliance draws attention to the extreme ideology's propagation among the youth of the nation, who are seen as its probable heirs to power. The future of our educational system and the values our children will be taught in light of this tendency is concerning and very problematic.

VIOLENCE AND BRUTALITY

A sobering reminder that violent extremist groups are gaining popularity is the awful arsenic attack on August 5th and the resulting horrible murder of innocent individuals. They are prepared to sow seeds of doubt and terror if it means achieving their goals. These savage crimes indicate a new low point, and things could get out of hand if we do nothing quickly.

DISORDER AND LAWLESSNESS

A terrifying new level of lawlessness has emerged as a result of recent political unrest. Criminals have seized the opportunity to engage in illicit activities with low fear of consequences while the government attempts to maintain control. Violence and intimidation have flourished as a result of the breakdown of law and order, which has far-reaching consequences. Students, previously regarded as beacons of hope and progress, are now frequently portrayed as criminals who participate in violent rallies and disrupt public order.

POLITICAL VICTIMIZATION

The political scene is increasingly marked by the silence of alternative voices. With the development of authoritarianism, many political activists and opposition leaders face persecution, jail, or worse. This political scenario of fear stifles healthy political discourse and degrades democracy, leaving citizens disillusioned and indifferent. The lack of a platform for political discourse leaves a need that extreme groups are eager to fill.

HISTORY AT STAKE

There is rising fear that the present generation of Bangladeshi students, inspired by radical ideas, is attempting to erase the country's independent history. It is possible that a story that glorifies bigotry and extremism would triumph over the fight for freedom and secularism. Bangladeshi culture has always been characterized by its values of plurality and coexistence; yet, this erasing of past threatens both national identity and those goals for the future. A future fraught with uncertainty keep going in this direction, and Bangladesh can wind up becoming "Afghanistan 2.0." A perfect storm threatening to devour the nation is created by the confluence of political instability, the proliferation of radical ideologies, and a failing economy.

THE UNCERTAINTY AND FUTURE

Imagine a world where intolerance, tyranny, and hatred are common, like the Taliban's Afghanistan. It's possible that, especially powerful ones like the US and India, must intervene quickly to address the Bangladesh problem. Bangladesh and the region are in danger and immediate action need to be taken to strengthen democratic institutions, preserve human rights, and resist extremism. Bangladesh has experienced 12 year highest inflation rate at 11.66 percent in July, which is the alarming situation for uncertainty in the country (Press Trust of India, 2024).

BANGLADESH TURMOIL AND INTERNATIONAL COMMUNITY

An immediate action becomes prerequisite to eradicate extremism and persecution, Bangladesh risks losing its democracy and prosperity, international community specifically India being it's neighbor and United States as world leader should take prompt action to avoid another Afghanistan experience. To stop this instability in Bangladesh, the US and India must act now, because Bangladesh's instability threatens India's geopolitics in South Asia. Moreover, US and India need to take swift and prompt action to avoid this turmoil in Bangladesh (Ahmede Hussain, 2023). The turmoil in Bangladesh pose direct threats for India's strategic and regional position in South Asia.

CONCLUSION

In summary with problems that can cause a retreat like Afghanistan's, Bangladesh is at a crossroads. There is a grave threat to the social and democratic principles of the nation because of economic hardship, political unrest, and the emergence of extremist groups. Now it's the high time for the international community to act and withstand with democratic values. It becomes share responsibility of the civic world to instill justice, freedom and equality in this nation of South Asia. Extremism and persecution that has been perpetrated by the contemporary government need to be stopped and democratic principles should be restored.

CHAPTER EIGHT

"POLITICAL INSTABILITY IN BANGLADESH AND DR. MUHAMMAD YUNUS"

Muhammad Yunus was born in Bangladesh, he is the one whom we know as the 'Banker to the Poor,' he was honored with Nobel Peace Prize in the year 2006 for establishing the Grameen Bank and coming up with the ideas of micro credit and micro finance. Thanks to him millions of poor people, particularly women, have been given an opportunity to get small loans that change lives and whole communities. In recent years, Dr. Yunus has experienced legal chases, political pressures and most recently Unglamorous entry to the Bangladeshi political theatre.

THE NOBEL LAUREATE AND LEGAL STRUGGLES

The award of the Nobel Prize to Dr. Yunus was a big boost that placed him on world map as a champion of economic inclusion. But then his success did not go without controversy or legal cases; especially from Bangladeshi leadership under Sheikh Hasina. It is discriminatory for him to be removed from the position of the managing director of Grameen Bank in 2011on some flimsy reasons such as age limitation. Most people attributed this action to political reasons especially due to conflict between Hasina and Yunus over his perceived political power and his opposition to government fraud.

These trials involved prosecution on issues such as tax fraud, corruption and other issues which were meant to bring the reputation of the president into disrepute. The internal and external opponents of the government saw what happened to Dr Yunus as an act intended to demoralize opponents as well as weakening Dr. Yunus who has been a very vocal critic of the government. However, after the removal of Ershad regime and other democratization processes in Bangladesh, Yunus remained as a front line activist of democracy, open society and reforms in Bangladesh.

ASSUMPTION OF POWER AND THE CURRENT POLITICAL CLIMATE OR ARENA

Suddenly, after the removal of Sheikh Hasina's government on August 5th, Dr. Yunus as the managing director of Grameen Bank stepped into politics. It is a period of shift and unpredictable transition currently evidenced by Bangladesh's leadership crises and escalating tension. There has been a lot speculation as to why the mild-mannered Dr. Yunus has suddenly emerged as the leader of the Grameen Bank saying that he might be a Trojan horse in the region serving the interests of the West or is an agent of change working for the improvements of the political systems of Bangladesh.

CONSPIRACY THEORIES AND SPECULATIONS

Political explanations on the emergence of Dr. Yunus as the leader of Grameen Bank bear the elements of the bipolar society in Bangladesh. Some sections of society have given this perception that his rise to power is the west's conspiracy to unseat Bangladesh government. Some people believe that his participation is as self-serving as he wants to benefit from the destruction of Hasina's government. These theories though lacking empirical data, show that in the country deceitfulness and polarization are instinctively installed as what defines the political system.

PATH TO STABILITY: SUGGESTION'S FOR DR YUNUS

The Prioritize Law and Order: For instance, the main objective which must remain the focus of Dr. Yunus is to reinstate law and order. Trust rebuilding process can only be possible in a stable and secure environment that has to be created for citizens and investors. Fighting increasing crime levels, minimizing politico-security threats and enforcing the rule of law are basic building blocks towards state stability.

❖ Engage All Political Parties: In this case, Dr. Yunus has to embrace the politics and get into contact with all the political parties, including the ones that may not be supporting him at all. This kind of mobilization will ensure that a large base of the society is involved, thus achieving the goal of unity in fighting political fragmentation.

- ❖ Set a Timeline for Elections: Dr. Yunus has to set clear timeline for the free and fair elections which will ensure peaceful transfer of power to the legitimate government. They will assist in legitimizing his leadership, unlike any coup or authoritarian actions, that could be perceived within I shunned.

- ❖ Build Trust Through Fairness: neutrality and fairness in dealing with people is something that goes a long way in winning the trust of the Bangladeshi people. He has to rid himself of any perceived prejudices and rule for the rights and freedoms of all the people irrespective of their politics.

- ❖ Ensure Impartial Justice: Another concern is the reforming of the judicial system with a view of being in a position to offer competent and fair justice. This is because the judiciary has to deliver its services without the intervention of politicians to increase the public's trust in the legal system.

- ❖ Protect Religious Minorities: After the toppling of Hasina government there have been revelations of escalating cases of attacks on the religious minorities. They surely are in a desperate need of this kind of help from Dr.Yunus and other NGOs so that the vulnerable groups remain under his protection since their safety defines Bangladeshi government's respect for human rights and democratic principles. This is because failure in the protection of the minorities would result in the destruction of the social fabric similar to what happened to Afghanistan.

❖ Address the Rise of Militant Islamic Groups: In Bangladesh, militant Islamic groups have emerged and are now enjoying operational freedom that makes the country's future very uncertain. A clear implication is that Dr. Yunus must act very decisively against any tendencies of extremism and this can only do by applying both precautionary measures as well as stern enforcement against these groups.

❖ Strengthen Strategic Relationships: Expansion of strategic partnerships will be a significant element in Bangladesh's geopolitics and it will have to focus on developing good relations with its immediate neighbors, India in particular. However, as a long-term strategy the current Bangladesh government will need to adopt a balanced foreign policy, which means that Dr. Yunus, much as he is a personal friend of the United States, will have to reign in his pro-Indian sentiments if he wants to maintain his relevancy in the South Asia region.

LESSONS FROM GEOPOLITICAL TURMOIL

The current status of Bangladesh has clear analogs in the list of other countries, affected by geopolitics like Pakistan, Sudan and Syria. In Pakistan due to the political instabilities; authoritarianism and mobilization of militant groups, democracy has been hampered and this has resulted to prolonged military rule. Similarly, the civil instabilities together with external interferences and political estrangement have as well kept Sudan as a nation that has never ever experienced political steadiness at one or the other times. Syria has plummeted into civil war as a result of this need to assert influence over it by regional and international players demonstrating that when extremism and authoritarianism are allowed to reign supreme the results can be terrible.

Even though for Dr. Yunus these examples raise questions of internal strife, adherence to rule of law and avoiding to turn into the playground of external powers. Neglecting it could see Bangladesh become unstable thus, exposed to the same devastating outcomes as some of the countries.

NAVIGATING GEOPOLITICS: THE ART OF THE PLATE PLATING

Although, the friendly relationship between Dr. Yunus and the United States must be an asset for some diplomacy, some aspects of the geopolitical implications are important to consider. The U. S. has its own appreciations for Bangladesh but it cannot compromise South Asian Geo Politics which is influenced by India. Dr. Yunus has therefore to manage these relations effectively; for close bilateral relations with India but act and operate concurrently with other countries of the region and the world.

CONCLUSION

Bangladesh's history is at the crossroads and Dr. Muhammad Yunus is the man who is now in the middle of that controversy, holding the tremendous responsibility to lead the nation in the troubled times. He shall stand for challenges that regard the resurrection of law and order, supremacy of the rule of law, politics of inclusion, protection of the vulnerable groups, and diplomacy of balancing power brokers. As we observed the case of other nations that have already gone through similar learning curves, while cherishing the principles of justice, fairness and democratic dispensation, he has every chance to develop a stable and prosperous Bangladesh. The challenges that lie ahead are numerous and, nonetheless, with strong determination as well as staying loyal to the principles set out by him throughout his career, Dr. Yunus will be able to build the framework for a stronger, united Bangladesh.

CHAPTER NINE

MINORITY REPRESENTATION IN PUBLIC SPACES: ANALYSIS OF LAST 100 DAYS

'Robi Das'

Mr. Barry Gardiner, a Member of British Parliament, during a question-and-answer session in the British Parliament said, "Since the fall of the previous government in August of this year, Bangladesh has seen more than 2000 incidents of violence most of which are targeted against the minority Hindu Community". His statement described the present situation of the Hindu religious minorities of Bangladesh almost correctly. The figure he mentioned was true up to 20 August 2024, according to a report of the Bangladesh Hindu Buddhist Christian Unity Council (BHBCUC). The situation got worse in the later days.

Hindus, irrespective of their age and gender, took to the streets after the fall of the Hasina government and demanded that the atrocities are stopped immediately, and the perpetrators are brought to justice. Despite their demand, the present interim government of Dr. Yunus, a Noble peace prize recipient, failed not only to curb the violence against the religious and ethnic minorities, but also failed to lodge any criminal cases against the perpetrators. Moreover, Dr. Yunus and his advisors started to deny the facts and figures. Interestingly, they said that 'Yes, some Hindus are attacked, but they are attacked because of their affiliation with Bangladesh Awami League'. They tried to downplay the numbers and to legitimize their failure. Moreover, the interim government gave indemnity to all the perpetrators who committed atrocities against the Hindus stating that every incident was committed as a part of the 'July revolution'. These initiatives gave them the chance to build a bridge with the fundamentalist Islamists who are anti-Hindu and anti – India, because they needed their support to run the government.

The result is the religious minorities, especially the Hindus, started to present their demands in public spaces, both on the streets and on social media. In this situation, most of the Hindu religious groups got together and formed an alliance known as 'Sonatan Jagaran Mancha' (the Mancha) and ISCON's Chinmoy Das became its voice in the public spaces. It should be noted that a good number of young people supported the Mancha and Chinmay Das. They were following him, not because all of them are ISCON followers, but they wanted him to tell the stories of discrimination in front of world so that their demands are met, so that they can enjoy human dignity and equal rights in Bangladesh. However, the interim government had other plans.

POLICIES AND PLANS OF DR. YUNUS GOVERNMENT TO CURB THE PUBLIC SPACE FOR MINORITY REPRESENTATION:

Dr. Yunus's government wanted to squeeze the voices of the Hindu populace in the public places by injecting fear in their mind. The government systematically planned to weaponize the police and the judicial system against the Mancha and those who raised their voice or may raise their voice. They took this strategy from the very moment they came into power. For example, the largest secular forum in Bangladesh is the Forum for Secular Bangladesh (the Forum) led by Shahriar Kabir, a journalist, author and film maker and a recipient of the Amnesty International Award. Being forced by the Islamists and in fear that the Forum may took to the streets against their jihadist islam's revival policy, the police arrested him on 17 September on a false murder case and till today he is arrested in another 7 cases. He is told that if the Forum does not protest the policies of the current government, there will be no more arrests, and he will not be taken into remand. A similar strategy was taken to silence the voice of Advocate Rana Das Gupta, the general secretary of BHBCUC, who is also accused in a false and fabricated murder case. Due to such weaponizing of the police and the judicial system, the activism and protests in public spaces of both the Forum and the BHBCUC are squeezed. When public spaces are not available, then three fundamental rights, i.e., freedom of assembly, freedom of association and freedom of expression,

are denied. That is the plan of the present Yunus
government.

To materialize this plan, a fabricated sedition case
was filed against Chinmay Das and some of his
followers. Then the government starts the 'cat and
mouse game'. At first, Chinmay Das was not
arrested, but a few of his followers were. The policy
makers of the current Yunus regime thought both
Chinmay Das and the Morcha would become silent.
The police took the strategy to test the water.
Generally, this kind of tactic does not work when
you do not cure the disease, rather want to suppress
the symptoms.

At first, the students during their movement in July
used cancel culture and denied that the Hindus are
patriots. They portrayed the Hindu populace as
Indian aficionados. As a result of that we see that
Hindu government officers were targeted after 5
August. Hindu police officers did not join in their
service, Hindu professors and teachers were forced
to resign when Mob attacked them and Hindu
officers working in the administration or judiciary
were posted to different places. The cancel culture
was used further by the government to deny
inclusion of any religious minority members in
different reform commissions.
By the end of September both Bangladesh Army
and Bangladesh Police launched a joint commission
for restoring law and order. However, they did not
launch any attack against the Islamists; rather they
attacked the Hindu inhabitants of Hazari goli of
Chattogram on 5 November 2011. To hide their
activities, they destroyed all the cctv cameras of that
area. Despite the allegations of human rights

violations, the Yunus government neither started any investigation nor filed any case against the Army or the Police officials.

The conviction that this part of the Yunus government's plan gets firm when you see from the media that the government did not investigate any of these incidents or bring anyone before the court for trial.

HOW DID THE BANGLADESH GOVERNMENT SHRED MINORITY REPRESENTATION IN THE PUBLIC SPACE:

The religious and ethnic minorities have not enjoyed freedom in making representations about their demands in public spaces for the last couple of decades. Continuous human rights violation is the main reason behind it. The main human rights violations the religious and ethnic minorities have experienced in Bangladesh over the years are:

- ❖ Constitutional inequality: Article 2A of the constitution declared 'Islam' as the state religion. Due to this Article, the people following other religions have become second class citizens.

- ❖ Land grabbing: The right to property, a fundamental right as per the constitution, is denied to the Hindu populace under the garb of Vested Property Act.

- ❖ Use of Digital Security Act: On 4 December 2024, a mob attacked the Monglargao village of Doyarbazar Police Station under Sunamganj alleging that Akash Das, a young Hindu of that village posted blasphemous statement on his Facebook page. The mob lynched him and his family and torched a number of houses of Hindu families. Later the police arrested Akash under the Digital Security Act, which this interim government promised to repeal.
- ❖ The Digital Security Act, a draconian enactment, has blasphemy clause and if anyone from the religious or ethnic minorities make any comment in public or private spaces (private space includes social media pages of an individual) against, however remote it may be, Islam, they are beaten up by the mob, arrested by the police or the army, and if they remain alive then they are taken into custody. The courts of Bangladesh do not grant bail to anyone who is accused of making blasphemous comments in any space. You may not find any lawyer to represent any person accused of making blasphemous comments.

There is evidence that Islamists quite often post derogatory words on social media and spread hateful comments in the name of Friday preaching. But the Bangladesh authority never filed a case against them under the Digital Security Act or the Penal Code for making blasphemous statements against the Hindu deities.

- ❖ Violence against religious and ethnic minorities: Whenever the religious and ethnic minorities made any demands or raised their voice against discriminatory treatment in public spaces, or even in private spaces, it has become a practice that religious fundamentalist mobs attack those groups or villages or towns where those groups or individuals live. The governments since independence in 1971 have continuously failed to bring the perpetrators to justice.

After the fall of Sheikh Hasina government on 5 August 2024, BHBCUC recorded more than 2000 incidents, including murder and rape, taking place within the first 15 days all around the country. Temples, Pagodas and Churches nothing was left untouched. Till the end of September it was the mob only who were attacking. But from the mid-September both the Army and the Police jointly attacked the religious and ethnic minorities. Before attacking Hajarir Goli, the joint forces along with Islamists attacked the ethnic minorities of the Hill tracts on 19 September and 20 September. The government again did not make any investigation of human rights violations committed by the joint forces and the Islamists.

The continuous atrocities against which the state is not taking any steps to stop, and, in many cases, the widespread and systematic nature of the crimes is indicating towards commission of crimes against humanity against religious and ethnic minorities of Bangladesh. Lemkin Institute in its statement on 24 September stated that the recent incidents against the Hindu populace of Bangladesh indicate towards the presence of genocidal elements. Due to this widespread violence, the minorities are living in fear and due to fear they are not able to express themselves in public space.

- ❖ Lack of representation: The present government led by Dr. Yunus has formed several commissions to reform the state and recently, he has formed the election commission. Unfortunately, you will not find members from religious and ethnic minority groups. This has affected minority representation in public space gravely and it is expected that the concerns of the minorities will not be presented before these commissions.

- ❖ Weaponizing court procedures by filing of mass criminal cases against community leaders, human rights defenders and human rights activists: After 5 August 2024, mass criminal cases are filed against community, human defenders and activists to shut their voices in the public spaces. A lot of them are arrested as well. Earler cases against Shahriar Kabir, Rana Das Gupta and Chinmay Pravu are discussed. On 28 November, the government filed 2 criminal cases against 84 Hindu lawyers of Chattogram Bar Association who represented Chinmay Das Pravu on 26 November. For these cases, out of fear none of the lawyers appeared on behalf of Chinmay Das during his bail petition hearing on 3 December. Moreover, one lawyer Rabindra Ghosh went to appear for Das. Both the police and the Islamist lawyers prohibited him from going into the court room. Due to using legal cases and court procedures as a weapon, thousands of community leaders and defenders are now silent and on the run.

❖ Culture of Impunity: Since independence, there is not a single case where any perpetrators are tried and punished for committing crimes against religious and ethnic minorities. For example, after every election, religious and ethnic minorities are the victims of post-election violence. Everyone knows who the perpetrators are, in spite of that they are never arrested or brought to justice. This has resulted in a culture of impunity. It is widely believed that the perpetrators who committed crimes after 5 August will also go unpunished. This has created a sense of fear among the minorities and due to this they do not feel safe in public spaces.

❖ Creating barriers for representation in public spaces: Recently on 22 November 2024, the Sonatoni Jagoron Moncho, were not allowed to hold their meeting in Rangpur Division at the designated place. They were forced to go to a rural place to hold the meeting. The participants were not allowed to stay in any hotel since the district administration issued orders so that they are not allowed to stay. Even bus associations were not giving buses or not taking any participants who were going to participate in the meeting. Finally, the present government heavily controlled both print and electronic media so that the news of the meeting do not circulate to the general people. This is the current picture of how minority presentation in public spaces is denied.

RECOMMENDATIONS

To ensure a safe and fearless public space for the minorities of Bangladesh, I make the following recommendations, which must be communicated to the government of Bangladesh:

1. Stop Violence and Bring the Perpetrators to Justice

- ❖ Halt all forms of violence against minorities immediately.
- ❖ Investigate all incidents through an independent inquiry committee and bring the perpetrators to justice.
- ❖ The present government can file cases before the International Crimes Tribunals of Bangladesh to address crimes against humanity and genocide committed after August 5, 2024.

2. Implement 8-Point Demands

- ❖ Establish an independent minority commission.
- ❖ Create a Ministry of Minority Rights.
- ❖ Enact the Protection of Minorities Act and establish an independent tribunal under this Act to try perpetrators.
- ❖ Enact the Religious Endowment Protection and Management Act and ensure proper implementation of the Vested Property Restoration Act.
- ❖ Establish separate land commissions for the ethnic minorities of the plain land and hill tracts.
- ❖ Enact the Anti-Discrimination Act without further delay.

3. **Stop Constitutional Amendment Process**

❖ Halt the current constitutional amendment process, which excludes participation from minority representatives and risks further discrimination against minorities.

4. Ensure Representation in Reform Commissions

❖ Include minority representation in all commissions established for state reform processes.

5. **Ensure Representation in State Organs**

❖ Guarantee proportional minority representation in state organs, including the national Parliament.

6. **Representation in the Election Commission**

❖ Ensure minority representation in the electoral process.

7. **Stop Culture of Impunity**

❖ End the culture of impunity and ensure justice for all minority victims who have suffered for decades.

8. **Stop Weaponizing Legal Instruments**

❖ Repeal discriminatory laws such as the Vested Property Act and Digital Security Act to ensure fair treatment of religious and ethnic minorities.

9. **Stop Weaponizing Judicial Procedures**

- ❖ Withdraw all cases against individuals like Shahriar Kabir, Chinmoy Pravu of ISKCON, and Advocate Rana Das Gupta.
- ❖ Release Shahriar Kabir and Chinmoy Pravu immediately.

10. Withdraw Fabricated Cases

- ❖ The international community must pressure the government to withdraw fabricated cases against secular leaders, human rights defenders, lawyers, and Hindu activists.
- ❖ Without such action, the fundamental rights of religious and ethnic minorities—such as the right to life, freedom of expression, and freedom of assembly—will be entirely lost in Bangladesh. Combined with the culture of impunity, this will create a fearful state for them.

THE YUNUS GOVERNMENT MUST REMEMBER THE WORDS OF ANDREW DOYLE:

"The mark of a healthy liberal democracy is that it is able to reach a consensus regarding civility without having recourse to criminalization or mob pressure to enforce such terms. The belief of the apparatchiks of Critical Social Justice—that all our problems will magically disappear once we outlaw certain points of view or words that cause 'harm'—is a utopian delusion."

The Yunus government must understand that
religious and ethnic minorities are citizens of
Bangladesh. They should not be subjected to witch-
hunting or be unfairly tagged with certain political
parties or countries. They have the right to support
any political party they choose. Excluding them
from public spaces is a clear violation of human
rights principles. The Yunus government must be
held accountable for shrinking minority
representation in public spaces.

CHAPTER TEN

WILL ALL HINDUS IN BANGLADESH BE DIMINISHED?

Dr. Delaware Arif and Dr. Nurun Nabi

With a fear of terrorist attacks, the United Kingdom government recently has updated its travel alert for Bangladesh. Assessing the current lawlessness and the rise of the religious fundamentalist groups after August 5, the UK government fears about indiscriminate terrorist attacks including crowded areas, religious buildings, and political rallies. The US State Department also has a similar travel advisory and asked Americans to reconsider traveling to Bangladesh. These are valid fears and the alerts from the two most powerful governments have substantial significance as the claims of both the UK and US governments are based on findings of the world-class intelligence of those countries.

We have observed that the current Interim Government led by Dr. Muhammad Yunus set hundreds of top terrorists and fundamentalists including Sweden Aslam, Picchi Hannan, and Shibir Nasir free from prison right after swearing off on August 8. Many of those terrorists and criminals were either on death row or serving lifetimes in prisons for crimes including killings and involving religious terrorists' activities. The attacks on Hindu minorities and burning down Hindu temples have become so frequent that ISKON which is known for its harmless Kirton, a religious and harmless chanting, has become a target by the people in power in Bangladesh. ISKON leader Bhramochari was arrested for so-called treasons.

These are a few examples of mayhem and lawlessness in Bangladesh and we rightfully predicted so in one of our published articles around a year ago. As lawful American citizens, we strongly believe that a democratic and peaceful Bangladesh would ensure the religious rights of all Bangladeshis and Bangladesh could be a strong partner of our beloved country the United States of America. Criticizing the missteps of the Bangladesh Awami League, we urged the US government to work for free and fair elections instead of supporting fundamentalist groups in the name of restoring democracy in Bangladesh. We also reminded the U.S. government that Awami League was a proven partner in fighting religious fundamentalism and thus ensuring the freedom of religion of all minorities in Bangladesh.

The international partners have acknowledged the importance of political stability in Bangladesh because of the geopolitical positioning of the country in the region and the Muslim world. Now, we have been suddenly observing the anti-judicial mob killings, and the political persecution of the leaders, and supporters of the Bangladesh Awami League and Jatiya Party, the two largest political parties that have support from more than half of the eligible voters, in Bangladesh.

However, the Yunus government is claiming that they are working towards a national consensus to make reforms in various sectors in Bangladesh. Recently, Dr. Yunus invited some of the political leaders except anyone from Bangladesh Awami League and Bangladesh Jatiya Party (Main Group). Now, the million-dollar question is: will the Interim government led by Dr. Yunus be able to make a meaningful consensus and reform excluding two major political parties in the name of not entertaining the so called fascists and their allies?

Both the Awami League and the Jatiya Party ruled the country more than two-thirds of the time after it gained independence in 1971. They have strong supporters and activist groups. Are those people going to sit idle while the student-run current government runs the steamrollers on the opposition? As a fact of the matter, the leaders and activists of both the Awami League and Jatiya Party will strike back and fight the supporters of the current government. As a result, we can see conflicts and fictions are obvious in the coming days and it is going to be more fierce and violent. There might be an ethnic cleansing against the Hindu minority groups as the supporters of the current government consider Hindus as the supporters of India or the collaborators of India and voters of Bangladesh Awami League.

The anti-Indian sentiment is at an all-time high among the activists and supporters of the current government in Bangladesh. The Hindus are being considered as the puppets of Bangladesh Awami League and the Indian government. As a result, many Hindus are being persecuted across the country and their leaders including Sonaton Jagoorn Manchu are under fire. Considering all of these, we can definitely predict an ethnic fight in the coming days in Bangladesh.

There might be a regional war between Bangladesh and India as most of the political leaders across the aisle in India have been demanding a surgical operation against the current government in Bangladesh. On the other side, supporters and policymakers of the current Interim Government are weighing in on a war against India. Recently, hundreds of former military officers who are members of the Retired Armed Forces Officers (RAOWA) marched on the street of the capital of Bangladesh, Dhaka, and mentioned that they could occupy Calcutta within hours in case a war broke out between India and Bangladesh. On the other hand, The Chief Minister of the neighboring Indian State Srimoti Mamata Bannerji already has demanded the presence of the UN peacekeepers in Bangladesh.

Rightfully, President-Elect Donald J Trump expressed his deepest concern regarding the situation in Bangladesh and the persecution of the Hindu minority in a Tweet right before the Presidential elections on November 3. The incoming NSA Director Tulsi Gabbard, a devotee ISKON fan, expressed the same concern in a video message. Echoing the voice of President Trump and top national security leaders, we urged the American government to read the writings on the wall and to reconsider the role of the U.S. in Bangladesh in stopping the rise of religious fundamentalism, protecting the minority Hindus, and the sake of the national interest of our beloved country the United States of America.

CHAPTER ELEVEN

FIRST 100 DAYS OF YUNUS REGIME

THE STORY OF THE RISE OF MILITANT ISLAMIST GROUPS IN A SECULAR BANGLADESH

By: Dr. Nurun Nabi & Rana Hassan Mahmud

On August 5, 2024, Bangladesh underwent a dramatic regime change. Following three weeks of student-led protests supported by radical Islamists, the military ousted Prime Minister Sheikh Hasina, forcing her to leave the country on a military plane. Since her exile, radical Islamic groups, including Jamaat-e-Islami, Hefazat-e-Islam, and Hizb ut-Tahrir—along with members of the Bangladesh Nationalist Party—have unleashed widespread violence against religious and political minorities, law enforcement agencies, and political activists.

This violence has resulted in the deaths of over a thousand members of the Bangladesh Police and individuals from minority groups.

ISLAMIST VIOLENCE AGAINST RELIGIOUS MINORITIES AND POLITICAL OPPONENTS

In the aftermath of Sheikh Hasina's ouster, Jamaat-e-Islami orchestrated attacks that destroyed 450 out of 639 police stations nationwide, killing thousands of police officers through brutal means such as burning, beating, and hanging, as reported by unofficial sources.

The events leading to Sheikh Hasina's ouster on July 15, 2024, appear to have been "meticulously planned," according to Mohammed Yunus.

The atrocities committed by Jamaat-e-Islami were reportedly inspired by strategies used by the Muslim Brotherhood during the ousting of Egyptian President Hosni Mubarak in 2011.

Dr. Yunus claimed in an interview with PRI that reports of attacks on Hindus were exaggerated, suggesting that the violence was politically motivated rather than communal. According to him, Hindus were targeted due to their perceived association with the ousted Prime Minister's political party.

These remarks, however, worsened the plight of Hindus and political activists. Furthermore, the Yunus administration later granted blanket immunity to those involved in the killings and destruction of public property between July 15 and August 8, 2024. This immunity is evidence of the regime's complicity in the July–August massacres.

MOHAMMED YUNUS'S GOVERNMENT LEVERAGING ISLAMIC MILITANTS

The Yunus administration has actively utilized the influence of Islamic militants. Mahfuz Alam, one of Yunus's special assistants, has alleged ties to the banned Islamist organization Hizb ut-Tahrir, which is prohibited in several countries, including Bangladesh, India, China, the U.K., and Germany.

Following his inauguration, Yunus facilitated the release of Jashimuddin Rahmani, a convicted member of the banned Ansarullah Bangla Team, an affiliate of al-Qaeda and its offshoot AQIS. Rahmani, convicted in 2015 for aiding in the murder of blogger Rajib Haider, had other terrorism cases pending against him.

Since the fall of Sheikh Hasina's government, radical Islamists have destroyed over 1,500 sculptures and murals, burned down the historic home of Bangladesh's Father of the Nation, and displayed contempt for cultural artifacts. Their actions echo the Taliban's destruction of the Buddhas of Bamiyan and ISIS's demolition of ancient archaeological sites.

POST-AUGUST 5 VIGILANTISM AGAINST POLITICAL OPPONENTS

In the three months following August 5, 2024, at least 715 people were killed, and approximately 11,000 were injured. Among the fatalities, 541 occurred in August, 84 in September, and 91 in October. An additional 84 deaths resulted from mob violence. These figures are based on reports from police, hospitals, and the Manobadhikar Shanksrikit Foundation (MSF).

Members of the ousted ruling party, Awami League, have faced severe persecution, including arrests, arson attacks on homes, and killings. Even the Jatiya Party, the last opposition party in parliament, has not been spared. Lawyers representing these political leaders face harassment, beatings, and arrests, signaling a collapse of the judicial system.

ATTACKS ON JOURNALISTS, ARTISTS, INTELLECTUALS, AND FREEDOM OF THE PRESS

Since August 5, the Yunus government has revoked the accreditation of 167 journalists deemed sympathetic to the former administration. Unsubstantiated allegations have been made against nearly 140 journalists, including prominent figures like Shahriar Kabir, Shomi Kaiser, and Shyamal Dutta.

Dr. Yunus, often seen as a pro-Western figure, has aligned himself with radical Islamist factions, posing significant risks to U.S. national security. This situation raises urgent questions: Why is Dr. Yunus collaborating with individuals linked to banned organizations such as ISIS, al-Qaeda, and Ansar al-Islam?

Allowing this crisis to persist will strengthen the foothold of virulent Islamist groups, potentially creating a launching pad for global terrorism.

CONCLUSION

Bangladesh's current situation is dire, with an unelected interim government led by Mohammed Yunus, backed by militant Islamist groups such as Jamaat-e-Islami. This regime's first 100 days have seen a rise in Islamist militancy, a breakdown of law and order, economic collapse, and shattered hopes for the country's future.

As per the constitution, Sheikh Hasina remains the legitimate Prime Minister of Bangladesh, as she has not resigned. An immediate return to constitutional governance is crucial to restore stability and safeguard the nation's future.

CHAPTER TWELVE

SITANGSHU GUHA, A COLUMNIST AN ADVOCATE FOR HUMAN RIGHTS HAS PRESENTED THE FOLLOWING STATEMENT AT THE GENEVA HRC-SR MINORITY FORUM

The 17th session of the UN Forum on Minority Issues.
HRC-SR Minority Forum, Geneva
28-29 November 2024

Honorable Chairman, Delegates, Friends, Good Morning!

It is my distinct honor and privilege to participate in this diverse forum. I last spoke in Geneva on 13th May 2003, urging the UN to address the alarming trajectory of Bangladesh, as it was moving toward becoming a monolithic theocratic Islamic state. At that time, I highlighted the plight of Hindus and other religious minorities. Twenty-one years later, on 29th November 2024, I stand here again. The population of religious minorities has dwindled from approximately 18% in 1970 to less than 9% in 2024. If this trend continues, Bangladesh will,

within a few decades, become a homogenous
Islamic country. Religious and ethnic minorities
will be forced to seek refugee status in other nations
as their rights are further eroded.

In the last 53 years, no government has taken
meaningful action to safeguard the lives and dignity
of religious minorities. Persecution has persisted
under every administration, including the recent
Awami League government led by Sheikh Hasina
and the current interim government headed by
Nobel Laureate Dr. Mohammed Yunus. No
government has taken steps to curb entities
sympathetic to Islamic militancy. Instead, they have
compromised with such forces for temporary
political gains, maintaining their grip on power.

During Sheikh Hasina's rule (2009–2024), the
world witnessed multiple attacks on Hindu lives and
properties. Homes and businesses were ransacked
and looted. On several occasions, Hindus were
killed, and Hindu girls were abducted, many of
whom were raped. None of these atrocities were
ever prosecuted in a court of law.

Since the collapse of Sheikh Hasina's government,
it has become evident that the new powers in
Bangladesh oppose the secularism enshrined in its
constitution. Efforts are underway to erase all
memories of the 1971 Liberation War and the
genocide committed by the Pakistani Army against
the people of Bangladesh. It appears that Islamist

forces aim to transform Bangladesh into a country governed by strict religious laws akin to those enforced in Afghanistan. Members of the interim government, including Dr. Yunus, often address minority communities, urging them to consider themselves full-fledged citizens rather than minorities. However, their actions consistently undermine the interests of these communities.

On 5th November 2024, in Hazari Lane, Chattogram, police and military personnel cordoned off the area, destroyed CCTV cameras, and brutally beat local Hindus in their homes. Hindu businesses were sealed, and many individuals were arrested, with more being targeted to this day. There are other cases where Hindu boys have been beaten to death or gravely injured based on false accusations of offending Islam.

The Bangladesh Army has been granted magisterial powers to oversee law and order. The Hazari Lane incident was conducted under the Army's command, signifying direct confrontation between the Army and the civilian population. In September 2024, this same Army targeted the ethnic Buddhist Chakma community in the Chattogram Hills, killing several individuals. Ironically, this is the same Army that participates in UN peacekeeping missions.

Meanwhile, Chinmoy Krishna Das, formerly a member of ISKCON (International Society for Krishna Consciousness) and now the spokesperson for Bangladesh's Hindu Unity Platform, has been arrested on unfounded charges of sedition. Despite his peaceful advocacy for an eight-point demand, including the enactment of a "Minority Security Act" to protect religious minorities, the authorities have refused to engage in dialogue. This crackdown has escalated tensions and violence against the Hindu community.

Notably, ISKCON, a global religious organization rooted in Bengal's ancient Gaudiya-Vaishnava tradition, has distanced itself from political associations by revoking Chinmoy Das's membership. While ISKCON maintains a strictly apolitical stance and promotes non-violence, Islamist groups allied with Bangladesh's interim government are pressuring for the organization to be banned. A coordinated smear campaign against ISKCON is currently active in the country.

In the aftermath of protests demanding Chinmoy Das's release, credible reports indicate that authorities, in collaboration with local thugs, have carried out violent attacks on Hindu-majority areas in Chattogram. This alarming situation has placed the community in severe peril. Additionally, media outlets in Bangladesh are under strict government oversight, leaving a dearth of reliable information from the ground.

Given the escalating violence and suppression of minority voices, we urgently appeal to the United Nations and the international community to intervene. I urge the United Nations and the international community to take immediate action to investigate the gross violations of minority rights in Bangladesh, demand the release of Chinmoy Krishna Das and all others unjustly detained, hold the Bangladesh Army accountable for its actions, and push for the adoption of legal safeguards, including a Minority Security Act, to protect the lives, dignity, and properties of religious and ethnic minorities.

The campaign against Hindus and other religious minorities in Bangladesh is a slow-moving pogrom. Often, it is disguised as land disputes or allegations of offending religious sentiments. Many in the majority community view religious minorities as vulnerable due to the lack of state protection, making it easy to threaten and seize their property. With the rise of extreme Islamic sentiment, this threat has escalated into an existential crisis. Bangladesh's only hope lies in reclaiming the pluralistic, secular democracy envisioned by its founders.

Let us not stand idly by as an entire segment of humanity is driven to extinction. Let us act now to save the minorities of Bangladesh, to save its soul, and to preserve the ideals of justice and equality.

Thank you.

Sitangshu Guha

29 November 2024.

WHAT HAPPENED AT HAZARI LANE IN CHATTOGRAM IS 'CRIME AGAINST HUMANITY'

Sitangshu Guha.

When security forces break a Closed Circuit (CC) camera and enter someone's home or business, the purpose of their operation is bound to be questioned. This is exactly what happened in Hazari Lane, a Hindu-dominated area in Chattogram. The Army and Police, along with a group of Islamists, attacked Hindu homes and businesses at night, blocking off the entire area.

How many were wounded or killed? Nobody knows for sure because no media outlet was brave enough to report the incident. Still, the cries of the Hindus in Hazari Lane, as well as those across Bangladesh, continue to demand justice. But will justice ever be served? It hasn't happened in the past, and given the current circumstances, there seems to be little hope that it will happen now. Why? Because in a Muslim-majority country like Bangladesh, the persecution and victimization of Hindus and other religious minorities are often ignored.

The attack happened on Tuesday, November 5, 2024. The next day, the Army held a press conference, claiming that acid had been thrown at them, though no solid evidence was provided. Security forces also reported arresting 89 Hindus, accusing them of being involved in the incident.

Meanwhile, a member of the Muslim community expressed concern, comparing the security forces' actions in Hazari Lane to the treatment of Rohingyas in Myanmar. He urged the government to engage in discussions with the Hindu community about their eight-point demands. These include calls for justice for attacks on religious and ethnic minorities and the enactment of laws to protect their rights.
On Friday, November 8th, following the Jumma prayer, a large procession led by militant Muslim groups took place in Chittagong. Participants openly chanted slogans such as, "Catch an ISKCON/Hindu, slit their throat." ISKCON (The International Society for Krishna Consciousness) is a religious organization that promotes non-violence and spiritual practices based on the ancient Gaudiya-Vaishnava tradition of Bengal. A coordinated campaign by Ilias Hossain from the USA, Pinaki Bhattacharya from France, and journalist Mahbubur Rahman in Dhaka has sought to demonize ISKCON and incite violence against the organization and Hindus in general. On November 6th, Charu Krishna Das, secretary of ISKCON Bangladesh, issued a statement affirming the organization's non-political stance and denying any involvement with the movement.

Despite the inflammatory nature of the statements by the militant groups, police made no arrests in connection with the incident. The Army stated that they remained neutral during the operation, but major questions remain unanswered: "Why were the CC cameras disabled before the operation?" and "Why were civilian cadres involved alongside security forces?"

We spoke with two eyewitnesses who were afraid to publish their names. They reported that 57 Hindus were injured. Initially, police detained about 200 Hindus, taking them to a nearby temporary military camp and keeping them isolated. Later, around 100 people were released. Police filed a case against 89 individuals, who were presented before a judge at 1 a.m. to avoid public attention. Eyewitnesses stated that the detainees had visible scars from torture, with some unable to stand in court. The witnesses also reported that they knew nothing about any "acid throwing," but they did observe stone pelting.

Earlier, it was reported that a Muslim man, Osman Mollah, posted something against ISKCON on social media, prompting protests from the Hindu community. Local Hindu and Muslim shop owners mediated the incident, and Osman issued a written apology, resolving the matter. However, militant groups were dissatisfied with this outcome and sought to punish the Hindus, who were organizing large protests. That night, militant Islamists, accompanied by police and military forces, launched an attack, looting 15–20 gold stores. Most of those arrested were innocent. Police identified businessmen like Rubel Saha, Amit Dhar, and Dr.

Kathak Das, who had no involvement, likely to
extort ransom from them.

Eyewitnesses reported seeing two factions within
the security forces—one entirely anti-Hindu and
another opposed to the raid on Hindu homes and
businesses. They also stated that Hizbut Tahrir and
Jamaat cadres joined the security forces and carried
out most of the looting.

They further reported that security forces continue
to raid Hindu homes. A young woman, Aradhya
Saha, filed a complaint with human rights defenders,
stating that she was home alone when security
forces and Jamaat supporters entered and ransacked
her house. Police have also continued to raid the
homes of activists involved in the movement. A
team from The Human Rights Congress for
Bangladesh Minorities (HRCBM), consisting of
Sumon Sikder, Laki Bacher, and Sujit Das, met
with the local police commissioner but received no
satisfactory responses.

According to sources, police questioned detainees
about a so-called RSS flag allegedly displayed
above the Bangladesh flag. In reality, it was a
saffron flag commonly used by Hindus, and the
other flag was not a Bangladesh flag. Police also
stated that they had never before seen so many
Hindus taking to the streets, asking whether India
was supporting them. They questioned why the
slogan "Jai Shri Ram" was used, viewing it as an
RSS slogan. However, "Ram" and "Krishna" are
two incarnations of God, and "Jai Shri Ram" and
"Hare Krishna" are common phrases among Hindus.
Reliable sources reported that an army team from

Dhaka would soon visit Chittagong to arrest members of the Bangladesh Hindu Jagoron Moncho involved in the movement. Police filed a case against Hindus, listing 49 arrested individuals and 500 unknown persons. The military may add to this list of 500. The main leader, Chinmoy Krishna Das, is also at risk of arrest. BNP leaders are trying to support Hindus and have requested Chinmoy Das to pause the movement, prompting him to declare a 15-day break.

The Chittagong Hill Tracts, a news portal, reported on November 7th that, since the evening of November 5, 2024, the Bangladesh Army, along with Border Guards Bangladesh (BGB) and local police, had launched a violent, targeted crackdown on Hindu-majority areas in Chattogram. Reports from victims and eyewitnesses in the region indicate that heavily armed soldiers, backed by paramilitary forces and police, have conducted door-to-door raids in Hindu neighborhoods, including Hazarigolli and surrounding areas. Security forces are accused of forcibly entering homes, rounding up all male residents, and taking them into custody under unclear circumstances. In a disturbing escalation, several reports claim that security personnel also destroyed CCTV cameras to prevent documentation of these actions.

The Global Bangladeshi Hindu Alliance alerted the world that "more than 80 Hindus were picked up at midnight as army and police surrounded the Hindu neighborhood of Hazari Lane in Chittagong." They reported that security forces ransacked homes and shops, destroying CCTV cameras to eliminate evidence, and beat Hindus mercilessly—women, children, and elderly alike. Many were severely injured. They also alleged that security forces tortured detainees during interrogation and warned that the Hindus would be charged under the non-bailable "Acid Throwing Act of 2002," carrying a potential death penalty. Hindus are comparing the Hazari Lane raid to the infamous "Black Night" of March 25, 1971, when the Pakistani army massacred Bengalis. Questions have been raised: "Are Hindus safe in the hands of the Army?" "Is this the Bangladeshi army or a Pakistani army?" and "Are these army and police officers part of the UN Peacekeeping Mission?"

CHAPTER THIRTEEN

EXISTENTIAL THREAT FACING BANGLADESH'S RELIGIOUS & ETHNIC MINORITIES AND ITS SECULAR DEMOCRACY

By Dwijen Bhattacharjya, Ph.D.

INTRODUCTION

The religious and ethnic minority communities of Bangladesh, along with its fledgling secular or pluralistic democracy, are facing an existential threat from the Islamists who effectively took control of the country on August 5, 2024, through a "meticulously designed" mass uprising. On September 25, 2024, Chief Adviser of the Interim Government, Dr. Yunus, said in his Clinton Global Initiative speech, as he introduced his Special Assistant Mahfuz Alam as the "Mastermind" (his own words) of the August 5, 2024, mass uprising that toppled Prime Minister Hasina's government, that it was a "meticulously designed" event.

The uprising forced Prime Minister Sheikh Hasina to abdicate power and flee the country. Although, on the surface, it appeared to be a student-led movement seeking the abolition of the civil service job quota for the descendants of the Freedom

Fighters of 1971, this highly consequential regime change was actually orchestrated. The student protest's original goal was to push the government to reduce the civil service quota for the descendants of Freedom Fighters. The government met their demand through a court order, and unless the movement had been morphed into a nationwide uprising to oust Prime Minister Sheikh Hasina's government, it would have ended there. The student coordinators themselves admitted that they had no plans to topple the government.

This regime change, however, was orchestrated by Islamic nationalists, fundamentalists, and extremists of Bangladesh, financially and logistically backed by an international network of Islamic terrorists, Pakistan's Inter-Service Intelligence (ISI), and global superpowers seeking unfettered access to the country for geopolitical reasons (Abhinandan Misra's article, Sunday Guardian, September 15, 2024; Chandan Nandy's article, Northeast News, September 6, 2024).

Over the years, world leaders, international think tanks, and media outlets have heaped praise on Sheikh Hasina for her stellar achievements in areas such as sustained economic growth, curbing Islamic terrorism, infrastructure and telecommunications development, women's educational and political empowerment, disaster management, infant mortality reduction, and poverty eradication. In sharp contrast, she also faced severe criticism since 2014 for her authoritarian behavior, rampant financial corruption, blatant cronyism, and political repression. Thus, not only did Hasina's Islamic political opponents and their international terrorist backers euphorically celebrate her sudden ouster, buoyed by the sure prospect of returning to power

as they did in 2001, but even some members of
Bangladesh's civil society hailed this regime change
as an opportunity for the people to establish a
political system free of cronyism, repression, and
corruption. This sentiment was reflected in media
reports of the time ("Bangladesh begins again,"
Economist, August 10–16, 2024).
However, the vast majority of the country's
moderate or progressive Muslims and the religious
and ethnic minority citizens—who historically
voted for the coalition of fourteen parties led by
Sheikh Hasina's Awami League because it was
secular-democratic, at least by its manifesto—
viewed this change as a cataclysmic disaster. They
knew that the mass uprising of August 5, 2024, was
executed by the joint forces of Islamic nationalists,
fundamentalists, extremists, and proscribed
militants. These forces now had no obstacle to
returning to power, ruling the country as they did
from 2001 to 2006, when Bangladesh resembled
Taliban-ruled Afghanistan.

The Awami League had established secular-
democratic Bangladesh in 1971 by leading the
nation through a genocide conducted by the
Pakistani army and their Bangladeshi Islamic
extremist allies like Jamaat-e-Islami. Over time,
however, the party formed alliances with 63 of the
country's 70 Islamic fundamentalist groups (Asia
Times, December 7, 2018), compromising the equal
rights of non-Muslim minorities and the secular-
democratic principles upon which the country was
founded. This foundation was built at the cost of
three million lives, the forced sexual slavery of an
estimated two hundred thousand women, and the
exodus of nearly ten million people—most of them

religious and ethnic minorities—to neighboring India amidst atrocities.

Since Bangladesh's only other major political party, the Bangladesh Nationalist Party (BNP), which ruled the country in the late 1970s, 1990s, and again from 2001 to 2006 (both by itself and in coalition with the Islamic extremist party Jamaat-e-Islami), is equally culpable of the same offenses and crimes that Sheikh Hasina's government has been accused of, the community of secular-democratic nations should now worry about the direction in which Bangladesh is headed.

WHAT NEXT FOR BANGLADESH?

Bangladesh has drifted far from the secular democratic principles upon which it was founded in 1971. The erosion of these values began in 1978 and culminated in 1988 when President H. M. Ershad declared Islam the state religion through the 8th Amendment to the Constitution, effectively licensing Islamists to pursue their goal of ridding the country of its non-Muslim population through violence. Despite this, the country maintained a semblance of secular democracy until August 4, 2024. However, the student "revolutionists" of August 5 and their Islamist backers are systematically erasing the last vestiges of secular democracy. Concurrently, a Constitution Reform Committee is working to amend the constitution to reflect "people's desire," as expressed through the mass uprising of August 5.

The most pressing question now is whether Bangladesh will remain the secular-democratic nation it was at birth in 1971 or revert to its pre-independence status as an Islamic republic. The following actions of the Interim Government provide clues about the country's direction:

i. On August 28, 2024, Dr. Yunus's government lifted the ban on Jamaat-e-Islami and its violent student wing, Islamic Chhatra Shibir. This organization opposed Bangladesh's independence in 1971, actively participated in the Bangladesh Genocide, vehemently opposed secular democracy and man-made constitutions, and openly declared its goal of transforming Bangladesh into an Islamic theocracy governed by Sharia law (The Daily Star, October 30, 2018).

ii. Dr. Yunus's government has allowed the international Islamic terrorist organization Hizb-ut-Tahrir, banned in many nations, including Bangladesh and the U.K., to operate freely within the country. On August 5, 2024, Hizb-ut-Tahrir destroyed the Holey Artisan sculpture Deepto Shapath (meaning "Firm Resolution"), which memorialized police officers killed during the containment of ISIL-inspired terrorists who massacred 20 people on July 1, 2016. The victims included nine Italians, seven Japanese, a U.S. citizen, and an Indian citizen.

iii. Dr. Yunus's government has released dangerous Islamic terrorists and convicted killers, including Jasimuddin Rahmani, the Chief of the banned terrorist organization Ansarullah Bangla Team (ABT), the Bangladesh chapter of Al-Qaida in the

Indian Subcontinent (AQIS). After his release, Rahmani called on West Bengal's Chief Minister, Ms. Mamata Banerjee, to declare independence from India.

iv. The August 5 "revolutionists" have destroyed over 1,500 sculptures and murals in the country (Prothom Alo, August 20, 2024). This includes the statue of the Nation's Founding Father, Bangabandhu Sheikh Mujibur Rahman, who created secular democratic Bangladesh in 1971 and enshrined equal rights for all citizens in the constitution, regardless of faith, race, or gender.

v. The "revolutionists" have destroyed nearly every sculpture related to the War of Independence, including in Meherpur, where the Declaration of Independence was made, and the sculptures of the seven Bir Sreshthas (Independence War heroes).

vi. The "revolutionists," who tore down the statue of Bangladesh's secular democratic Founding Father, observed the first-ever death anniversary of Pakistan's Founding Father, Muhammad Ali Jinnah, in Dhaka (Dhaka Tribune, September 12, 2024). This act signals the intent to revert Bangladesh to its pre-independence status as an Islamic republic.

vii. The current Attorney General of Bangladesh, Mr. Asaduzzaman, has called for the removal of secularism and Bengali nationalism from the constitution (The Economic Times, November 14, 2024).

For decades, Bangladeshi Islamists have openly declared their goal of establishing a Caliphate in

Bangladesh (The Daily Star, April 7, 2013;
International Business Times, October 30, 2014).
To achieve this, they have waged a systematic
campaign of religious and ethnic cleansing with
direct government complicity, particularly during
the BNP and BNP-Jamaat-e-Islami rule. This
vicious campaign persists under Dr. Yunus's Interim
Government as well Protected by total impunity, the
Islamist backers of the August 5, 2024
"revolutionists" continue their brutal persecution
and atrocities against the country's religious and
ethnic minorities. The following examples provide a
glimpse into the horrendous, unilateral sectarian
violence inflicted on Bangladesh's minorities:

In a press conference held in Dhaka, the Bangladesh
Hindu, Bouddha, Christian Oikya Parishad reported
alarming incidents of violence against religious
minorities—primarily Hindus—between August 5,
2024, and August 18, 2024. A staggering 2,010
incidents were recorded, impacting 1,705 families.
These included 915 cases of attacks, looting,
vandalism, and arson. Among these, 157 families'
homes and businesses were attacked, looted, and set
ablaze, 34 of which belonged to indigenous peoples.
Sixty-nine places of worship were vandalized,
looted, or burned down. Additionally, 38
individuals were tortured, four women gang-raped,
and nine murdered (Ekattor TV, September 19,
2024).
On September 20, 2024, 200 houses belonging to
indigenous peoples in Dighinala, Chittagong Hill
Tracts, were burned down, resulting in the death of
four individuals (The Daily Star, September 19 &
20, 2024).

On November 6, 2024, the armed forces and police jointly brutalized Hindus in Hazari Golli, Chittagong, who had gathered to protest a derogatory Facebook post by a local Muslim trader labeling ISKCON as a terrorist group. The authorities destroyed CCTV footage to conceal the brutality, leaving the exact number of casualties and injuries unknown. Shockingly, instead of apprehending the perpetrators, Dr. Yunus's government arrested 89 Hindu victims (bdnews24.com, November 6, 2024).

Islamists have openly threatened to massacre every member of the Vaishnav sect of Hinduism (ISKCON) unless the government bans the organization (Sangbad Protidin, November 15, 2024).

On November 25, 2024, a Hindu monk, Chinmoy Krishna Das, was arrested on fabricated charges of sedition. Denied bail, he was left without legal representation as Islamists used loudspeakers to threaten any lawyer who dared to defend him. Additionally, hundreds of minority officers and educators have been forced to resign solely because of their religious identity. The latest victim of this systematic purge is Dr. Anupam Sen, Vice Chancellor of Premier University in Chittagong (The Daily Star, December 7, 2024).

These atrocities have occurred under the watch of Chief of Army Staff General Waker Uz-Zaman and Chief Adviser Dr. Muhammad Yunus. Despite their capacity to intervene, both leaders have failed to act. Instead of addressing these grave issues, Dr. Yunus and his deputies have dismissed them as "overblown" and raised irrelevant questions such as why Indian media is reporting them or why Bangladeshi minorities are vocal now, ignoring a history of protests both within and outside the country, including during the October 2021 pogrom. The masterminds behind the August 5, 2024 uprising, Mahfuz Alam and Adviser Nahid Islam, have explicitly stated their intention to connect the events of 1947, 1971, and 2024. Their aim is to redefine Bengali nationalism, replacing the secular and inclusive identity rooted in the 1952 Language Movement with a Muslim Bengali nationalist identity that excludes non-Muslims. By excluding the principles of secular democracy enshrined in the 1972 Constitution, they aim to pave the way for an Islamic democracy, ultimately establishing a Majlis-E-Shura.

The international community is puzzled by Nobel Peace Laureate Dr. Muhammad Yunus's apparent complicity in transforming secular-democratic Bangladesh into an Islamic state. Several factors may explain his actions. First, as Dr. Yunus himself stated, he was "hired" by the student coordinators of the August 5 uprising and is bound to comply with their demands to avoid removal. Second, he may be seeking to evade the legal cases brought against him by the Hasina government, some of which carry heavy financial penalties and prison terms. Third, many believe Dr. Yunus's personal political convictions align with the Islamist backers of the uprising, as evidenced by his unprecedented visit to the Language Martyrs' Monument and the National Martyr's Memorial only after assuming office—protocol-driven acts that contrast starkly with the reverence these monuments command as symbols of secular Bengali identity and the sacrifices of 1971.

Disturbingly, Dr. Yunus excluded all progressive political parties, including the Awami League, from recent dialogues with political parties. Election Commission Reform Committee Chairman Badiul Alam Majumder and several government advisers have categorically stated that these parties, representing at least 50% of moderate or progressive Muslims and over 17 million minorities, will be barred from participating in the next election. This exclusion makes it almost certain that the BNP, either alone or in coalition with Jamaat-e-Islami, will secure an absolute majority, replicating their 2001 victory. Should this happen, Bangladesh risks becoming another Afghanistan, with its religious and ethnic minorities facing imminent extinction, a scenario predicted as early as 2016 by Professor Abul Barakat, who warned that "no Hindus will be left [in Bangladesh] after 30 years" (Dhaka Tribune, November 20, 2016).

MINORITY EXODUS AND DECLINE IN POPULATION REPRESENTATION

The alarming decline in the representation of minorities in Bangladesh's population is a direct result of escalating violence and persecution. Congressman Robert Dold, citing Professor Sachi Dastidar's research (Empire's Last Casualty: Indian Subcontinent's Vanishing Hindu and Other Minorities, 2008), reported to Congress that 49 million Hindus were "missing" from Bangladesh's minority population since 1947. Similarly, Bangladeshi human rights activist Priya Saha informed former U.S. President Donald Trump

during the 2019 IRF Ministerial that 37 million minorities had disappeared since 1971.
This exodus has led to a steady decline in the percentage of minorities within the country's total population. While minorities constituted 20% of the population in early 1971, they accounted for only 8.96% in 2022 (Bangladesh Census Report 2022). The indigenous peoples in the Chittagong Hill Tracts region, predominantly Christians and Buddhists, have seen their population percentage drop from 98.6% in 1947 to just 49% by 2023.

If not for the ongoing violence, forced displacement, and systematic persecution, Bangladesh's minority population would have reached 70 million today. However, only 17 million remain, leaving 53 million "missing" individuals, according to Professor Dastidar. Economist Professor Abul Barakat has predicted that "No Hindus [or other minorities] will be left in Bangladesh in 30 years" if the current rate of exodus persists (Dhaka Tribune, November 20, 2016).
Since the violent upheaval of August 5, 2024, which triggered a nationwide campaign of religious and ethnic cleansing, the situation has only worsened. Reports from both national and international media have documented these atrocities:

- ❖ "Hindus Under Attack! Minority Facing Ethnic Cleansing in Bangladesh" (Neo Politico, August 5, 2024)
- ❖ "Hindus in Bangladesh Face Revenge Attacks After Prime Minister's Exit" (The New York Times, August 7, 2024)
- ❖ "Hindus in Bangladesh Try to Flee to India Amid Violence" (Reuters, August 8, 2024)

- ❖ "200 Houses, Shops Set on Fire at Dighinala" (New Age, September 19, 2024)
- ❖ "4 Killed in Khagrachari, Violence Spreads to Rangamati" (The Daily Bangladesh, September 21, 2024).

Today, Bangladesh's minorities live in constant fear of torture, rape, eviction, or murder—circumstances eerily reminiscent of the genocide of 1971. This has been noted in international discussions such as H. Res. 1430 (Recognizing the Bangladesh Genocide of 1971, Rep. Steve Chabot, October 14, 2022) and documented in The Blood Telegram: Nixon, Kissinger, and a Forgotten Genocide by Gary J. Bass (2013).

ISLAMISTS' VISION: ESTABLISHING A CALIPHATE

For over three decades, Islamic hardliners in Bangladesh have openly expressed their goal of transforming the country into a caliphate, akin to ISIL. Their aspirations include expanding this Islamic state by annexing regions of neighboring India and Myanmar (TIME Online Edition, October 14, 2002; The Daily Star, April 17, 2013).
A notable attempt to implement this vision occurred on April 6, 2013, when Hefazat-e-Islam, supported by Islamist allies like BNP and Jamaat-e-Islami, mobilized hundreds of thousands of madrassa students to march on Dhaka. Their aim was to overthrow Sheikh Hasina's elected government and establish an Islamic state (The Daily Star, April 7, 2013).

Under the current interim government led by Dr. Muhammad Yunus, the Islamists have accelerated efforts to realize their objectives. This shift is evident in headlines such as:

❖ "Bangladesh Marching Towards Islamic Rule: Hifazat-e-Islam Calls for Destruction of Statues" (Neo Politico, August 17, 2024).
❖ "The Country Could Fall Prey to Islamic Extremism, as Pakistan Was" (The Economist).

The Islamists' gradual implementation of their agenda under Dr. Yunus's leadership has raised serious concerns about the future of secularism and democracy in Bangladesh.

THE NEXT PARLIAMENTARY ELECTIONS AND THEIR IMPLICATIONS

The next parliamentary elections in Bangladesh are poised to exclude progressive and secular political parties, marking a significant departure from democratic norms. Student Coordinator-Advisers of the interim government, including Mr. Nahid Islam, have labeled the Awami League (AL) as a "fascist" party and declared it ineligible to participate. Dr. Badiul Alam Majumder, Head of the Electoral System Reform Commission, reaffirmed this stance, stating that "elections without AL won't be considered unacceptable" (Dhaka Tribune and Business Standard, September 14, 2024). Without international intervention, the interim government under Dr. Yunus is likely to bar all 14 progressive parties from the elections. This

exclusion would pave the way for Islamic
nationalists and extremists to return to power with
an overwhelming majority.
The implications of such an outcome are dire.
Bangladesh risks devolving into an authoritarian
Islamic state, resembling Afghanistan under Taliban
rule. The religious and ethnic minorities, already at
the brink of extinction, would face even more
intense persecution and violence.

WHAT WILL BANGLADESH LOOK LIKE IN THE EVENT OF A RADICAL ISLAMIST -BNP COALITION VICTORY?

Here is what Bangaldesh looked like during their
last tenure in power in the 1990s or between 2001
and 2006:

- ❖ Bengali speaking Islamic jihadists fought in
  Afghanistan alongside Al-Qaida led by Bin
  Laden, and the Pakistanis, reported America
  Taliban John Walker Lindh to CNN (July 05,
  2002).
- ❖ "In Bangladesh, as in Pakistan, a Worrisome
  rise in Islamic Extremism," (WSJ, April2, 2002)
- ❖ "Bangladesh: A Cocoon of Terror", Far Eastern
  Economic Review, April 8, 2002).
- ❖ BNP & Jamaat- E- Islami government provided
  shelter to 400 or so the Afghan War veterans
  (TIME, Oct. 14, 2002).
- ❖ "Seven people have been killed in two bomb
  explosions at a music festival in the town of

Jessore in southern Bangladesh." (BBC News, March 07, 1999).

❖ "On August 17, 2005, in an unprecedented scale of terror attacks, Jamaat- Ul- Mujahideen Bangladesh (JMB) near simultaneously exploded 459 bombs in 63 out of the country's 64, killing two and injuring more than 120. The blasts hit sixty-three of the nation's sixty-four districts, targeting government buildings and train stations and sending waves of alarm across south Asia" (Council on Foreign Relations, August 29, 2005; The Daily Star, August 18, 2005).

❖ "In broad daylight of August 21, 2004, Islamist militants launched a heinous grenade attack on a rally of the then opposition Awami League at Bangabandhu Avenue in Dhaka. 24 people were killed and over 400 injured." (The Daily Star, August 21, 2004).

❖ On December 8, 2005, a suicide bomber of the banned militant organization JMB carried out the suicide bomb attack at the Netrakona Udichi office killing eight persons including, two front ranking Udichi leaders, and injuring 50 people." (Bangladesh Post, December 10, 2023).

The magnitude of the atrocities conducted against the country's religious and ethnic minorities can be easily gauged from the following media captions/reports:

❖ On April 10, 1992, when the indigenous people of Logan , Chittagong Hill tracts were preparing to celebrate their New Years' Day, Prime Minister Begum Zia of BNP sent the paramilitary forces to aid the Muslim settlers to conduct a massacre in which 600 to 800 Buddhists and Christian indigenous peoples were systematically executed before burning doe their entire village and then leveling it off with bulldozers (See, e. g., the Congressional letter of strong concern signed by seventeen U. S. Congresspersons issued on November 13, 1992).

- ❖ On June 3, 1997, In Baniar Char in the district of Gopalgonj, they bombed a Catholic church during the Sunday mass killing 10 people and injuring 20.
- ❖ On April 28, 1998, the Islamists destroyed and desecrated the statue of Virgin Mary and set ablaze the crucifix at St. Francis Xavier's High School in Dhaka.
- ❖ "Rape and torture empty the villages," The Guardian, July 21, 2003.
- ❖ "Bangladesh's religious minorities: safe only in the departure lounge" (The Economist, Nov. 29, 2003).
- ❖ 200 Hindu women in Char Fashion, Bhola in single spot in one night. The cadres of the Islamist BNP and Jamaat-E- Islami celebrating their election victory by mass-raping "two hundred women – "So, the loathsome thing happened, the Muslim men aped Hindu women… The village was sprinkled with the bodies of molested women, numb with pain and shock in the aftermath of nightlong abuse. They were beaten, bitten, scratched, pummeled, dragged and ravished." They were raped in the rice paddy, in the bush, on the river-bank, in their houses, and in the open field by gangs of men…" in one night in Char Fashion of Bhola,

and among them were an eight-year-old girl, a middle-aged amputee, and a seventy-year old woman" on a single spot (Badrul Ahsan, The Daily Star, Nov.16, 2001).

❖ "98% of the reported cases of rape victims belonged to the minority communities (The Daily Janakantha, Feb. 17, 2002).

❖ "11 Hindus Burned Alive in Banshkhali, Chittagong," The Bangladesh Observer, Nov. 29, 2003).

With the fusion of thousands of Al-Qaida and ISIS-trained Iraq and Syrian war veteran jihadists into the Bangladesh's Islamist forces comprised of the Islamic nationalist party of BNP and 70 or more Islamic fundamentalist, extremist, and militant groups, who toppled the government of Prime Minister Sheikh Hasina on August 05, '24, are significantly more powerful than they were in the 1990s and early 2000s.

The following media captions or reports should give the non-Soth Asia observers a good sense of how potent Bangladesh's Islamists are today, and, thus, what they might do if they are back in power:

On 07/01/2016. seven assailants, including suicide bombers, armed with grenades, firearms, and sharp weapons attacked the Holey Artisan Bakery in Gulshan neighborhood, Dhaka, Bangladesh. Two police officers, and at least 20 hostages were killed while the remaining 13 hostages were rescued after security forces stormed the bakery on July 2, 2016. The Islamic State in Bangladesh claimed responsibility for the attack. Sources also attributed the attack to Jama'atul Mujahideen Bangladesh (JMB) and Al-Qaeda in the Indian Subcontinent." (https://www.start.umd.edu/gtd/search/IncidentSummary.aspx?gtdid=201607010001).

Since September 2012, when in Ramu, Cox's Bazaar, 25,000 (twenty-five thousand) of the Islamists rampaged through 18 Buddhist and Hindu villages during which they burned down homes, temples, violated women, and brutally tortured the Hindus and Buddhists. (See, e.g. ABC TV, Sept. 30, 2012. Rioting mob torches temples in Bangladesh - ABC News).

Bangladesh: Deadly Attacks on Hindu Festival – 4 Dead After Police Shoot Live Ammunition into Crowd (HRW, Oct 21, 2021).

"3,710 attacks on Hindu community in last 9 yrs" (The Daily Star, October 19, 2021).

THE MISSED OPPORTUNITY

Prime Minister Hasina's policy of appeasing the Islamists allowed them to consolidate their power and gradually intensify their vicious campaign of religious & ethnic cleansing, and finally her government on August 05, 2024. Upon returning to power in 2009 with an absolute majority through an internationally lauded free and fair election, Prime Minister Hasina could have reinstated the 1972 constitution and thus restore secular democracy. Instead, she forged new partnerships with the Islamists, specifically Hefazat- E- Islam. To appease them, she granted every wish that the

Islamists ever made at the expense of the equal rights of the religious and ethnic minorities and secular democratic values. She also constitutionally re-affirmed Islam as the state religion (15th Amendment) and allowed the police and judiciary to arrest and incarcerate the minorities under the Digital Security Act whenever the Islamists falsely accused them of "insulting Islam or the Prophet," by hacking into their Facebook accounts or creating fake ones. Prime Minister Hasina's Government's promoted Salafi Islam with Saudi fundings which all but completely changed the linguistically based Bengali nationalist identity of the Bengalis in favor of a Muslim Bengali identity. In recent years, Prime Minister Hasina built 560 mega mosques[Like her father and Founding Father of the nation Bangabandhu Sheikh Mujibur Rahman, who established an Islamic Foundation through legislation in 1974 but not for the Hindus, Buddhists or Christians, Prime Minster Hasina also only built hundreds of mosques but not a single temple, pagoda, or church in the country.] and 8 iconic mosques around the country, promoted Qwami madrassahs rather than building regular public schools, and permitted unregulated waaz (Islamic sermon given to massive gatherings) in which the clerics routinely denigrated the non-Muslims by comparing the non-Muslims to animals, dog pee and poop, and encourage the common Muslims to grab their property, use their women for gratification, convert them to Islam by force, and even "remove" them if anyone stand in the way of spreading the message of Allah. This has had a significant impact on the erosion of secular democratic values in the country, paving the way for the Islamists to quickly accomplish their goal with the assistance of Dr. Yunus' Interim government.

FAILURE OF U. S. POLICY OF INTEGRATING THE ISLAMISTS INTO MAINSTREAM POLITICS.

The U. S. Department of State has always pursued a policy of integrating Bangladesh's Islamic fundamentalist and extremist politicians into national politics, but that policy failed because Jamaat-E- Islami has not only consistently refused to apologize for participating in the 1971 genocide, but also refused to recognize the man-written secular democratic constitution of the country, the people as the supreme source of power, and in the undisputed power of the elected officials to make laws. Like the ISIS, AL Qaida extremists or the Talibans, the Islamists of Bangladesh, also do not believe in democracy, they believe in Majlish-e-Shura; they do not believe in equal rights of all religious groups, they believe in Islamic supremacy; they do not believe that men and women are co-equal partners, they believe a woman's job is to bear children and raise them; and, they do not believe that men and women have the same right to education and work. In addition, they oppose all the finest of human achievements: science, fine arts, music, photography, movies, dance, music, music, music, sculpture, individual freedom, freedom of speech, or freedom of religion. Bangladesh's Islamists have publicly declared that that women are just an object of man's libidinous gratification,

and that women in the workforce are committing
zena (sexual sin). Above all, the Islamists do not
consider the non-Muslims any better than animals
and treat them as such.

WHAT DOES THE FUTURE HOLD FOR BANGLADESH?

If the community of civilized democratic nations
simply stand by as Dr. Younus and his "Student
Coordinator"-Advisers, acting under the dictations
of the Islamists, prepare to hold the next
parliamentary elections excluding all the relative
progressive political parties, who represent more
than 50% of the nation's voters, the Islamists will
certainly win like the Islamic Salvation Front of
Algeria or the Islamic Brotherhood of Egypt did,
and then deal with them like they dealt with the
Islamic Salvation Front or Muslim Brotherhood.
They must deal with the situation either now nor
after the election in their own interest; neither
America nor the E.U. nations or the democratic
South Asian nations can afford a nation of 171
million people go Taliban. It would be wiser, of
course, to deal with the situation now rather than
later. That could be accomplished by persuading
BNP to sever ties with Jamaat-E- Islami and its
three dozen or extremist allies including its
ferocious student front, Islamic Chhatra Shibir, as
has been called on by the E. U. and American
Congressman Jim Banks (House Res 160, February
28, 2019), allow all the political parties including
Awami League to participate in the election like the

Caretaker government of Dr. Fakhruddin did in 2008. If the competing geo-political interests of the superpowers in the Saint Martin Island - Cox's Bazaar region do not interfere with it, then this is an easily attainable goal because B.N.P. leadership is composed of tolerant Muslims who use Islam only as a political tool for winning elections, and Chief Adviser Dr. Yunus is friends with powerful American politicians. The big question though is: Would the U.S. government do it right this time? The United States stand for two things: democracy and human rights. In 1971, the people of Bangladesh won a parliamentary election conducted by the Pakistani army and won it. When the Pakistani military dictator inflicted a genocide on us rather than transferring power to the victorious party, Awami League, led by Bangabandhu Sheikh Mujibur Rahman, the United States helped Pakistan conduct the genocide in which they, together with their Bangladeshi ally Jamaat-E- Islami, killed 3 (three) million unarmed civilians, subjected over 200,000 young women to sex-slavery and forced nearly ten million progressive Muslims, Hindus, Buddhists, and Christians to flee to India as refugees. Now Bangladesh is faced with a very similar situation, and only time can tell how the United States will act this time around. On September 14, 2021 Joseph Allchin in his article titled "Battle for Bangladesh: Fifty years after independence, a nation founded on secular principles is still grappling with religious extremism,(https://newhumanist.org.uk/articles/585 1/the-battle-for-Bangladesh) wrote: The community of civilized nations cannot afford to lose this battle in its own interest. Indeed, protecting secular or pluralistic democracy in Bangladesh is a highly

desirable goal for the civilized democratic nations
in their own interest. Banladesh can potentially
remain a secular-democratic nation like any
civilized democracy in the world because the vast
majority of its citizens are moderate Muslims who
believe in a harmonious co-existence with people of
all faiths. Therefore, echoing the South Asia and
East Asia scholar and journalist, Selig Harrison, I
would like to conclude with the appeal, "Get a grip
on Dhaka, and do not write off secular democracy
in Bangladesh yet (Selig Harrison, L.A. Times, July
02, 2008).

CONCLUSION

Bangladesh's secular democracy is at a critical
juncture. Immediate action from the international
community is vital to support inclusive elections
and preserve the nation's pluralistic identity. The
future of Bangladesh depends on the collective
resolve of its people and the global community to
uphold secular democratic principles.

REFERENCES

Al Jazeera. (2024). Bangladesh Protests: What's Behind the Unrest?. Retrieved from https://www.aljazeera.com/news/2024/7/16/banglad esh-protests-whats-behind-the-unrest.

Al Jazeera. (2024). Bangladesh's Garment Sector Faces Political and Economic Instability. Retrieved from https://www.aljazeera.com

Al Jazeera. (2024). Bangladesh's Political Crisis: Regional Implications and Domestic Turmoil. Retrieved from https://www.aljazeera.com

Amnesty International. (2024). Bangladesh: Targeted Violence and Repression under Yunus Government. Retrieved from https://www.amnesty.org

Asia Society. (2024). Bangladesh's Political Turmoil and Regional Implications. Retrieved from https://asiasociety.org

Asia-Pacific Research. (2024). What's Behind Regime Change in Bangladesh?. Retrieved from https://www.asia-pacificresearch.com.

Bangladesh Rural Council. (2021). Good governance issues in Bangladesh: Challenges and options. Retrieved from https://rc.gov.bd/jss/wp-content/uploads/2021/09/5.-Good-Governance-Issues-in-Bangladesh-Challenges-and-Options.pdf

Bangladesh Think Tank Forum. (2024). From tension to terror: A socio-political analysis of Bangladesh under interim governance. Dhaka: Bangladesh Think Tank Forum.
bdnews24.com. (2024). Bangladesh's Political Transition and Economic Future.

BHBCUC. (2024). Reports on Sectarian Violence and Human Rights in Bangladesh. Published by the Bangladesh Hindu Buddhist Christian Unity Council.

Britannica. (2024). Bangladesh - Politics, Economy, and Society. Retrieved from https://www.britannica.com.

Carnegie Endowment. (2024). Bangladesh's governance crisis: What's next?. Retrieved from https://carnegieendowment.org

Dhaka Tribune. (2024). Bangladesh under Yunus: Reforms, Controversies, and Challenges. Retrieved from https://www.dhakatribune.com/bangladesh/365428/yunus-grand-conspiracy

Dhaka Tribune. (2024). Protests Escalate under Yunus: Civil Society Demands Elections. Retrieved from https://www.dhakatribune.com

DW News. (2023). Why is Bangladesh cracking down on Nobel laureate Yunus?. Retrieved from https://www.dw.com/en/why-is-bangladesh-cracking-down-on-nobel-laureate-yunus/a-66744299

Financial Times. (2024). Bangladesh Faces Investor Confidence Crisis Amid Political Unrest. Retrieved from https://www.ft.com

Financial Times. (2024). Bangladesh Struggles to Address Economic Challenges Under Interim Government. Retrieved from https://www.ft.com/content/bangladesh-economic-struggles

Financial Times. (2024). Economic Instability Fuels Protests in Bangladesh under Yunus. Retrieved from https://www.ft.com

Frontline. (2024). Muhammad Yunus: 'Banker to the poor' embroiled in battle for integrity. Retrieved from https://frontline.thehindu.com/news/profile-muhammad-yunus-banker-to-the-poor-embroiled-in-battle-for-integrity-sheikha-hasina-political-persecution-grameen-bank/article67702802.ece

Human Rights Watch. (2024). Bangladesh: Events of 2023. Retrieved from https://www.hrw.org/world-report/2024/country-chapters/bangladesh.

Human Rights Watch. (2024). Bangladesh: Human Rights Under Interim Government. Retrieved from https://www.hrw.org

Human Rights Watch. (2024). Bangladesh: Reports of Human Rights Violations under Interim Government. Retrieved from https://www.hrw.org

Human Rights Watch. (2024). Bangladesh: Violence and Rights Violations Under Interim Government. Retrieved from https://www.hrw.org/world-report/2024/country-chapters/bangladesh

International Finance. (2024). Economic Challenges in Bangladesh's Transitional Government. Retrieved from https://internationalfinance.com

IPS Journal. (2024). Bangladesh's Path to Democratic Stability: A Herculean Task. Retrieved from https://www.ips-journal.eu

Jahan, R. (1974). Bangladesh in Transition: Nation Building and Leadership. Dhaka: University Press.

Maniruzzaman, T. (1975). Bangladesh: An Unfinished Revolution. Journal of Asian Studies, 34(2), 238-259.

NobelPrize.org. (2006). The Nobel Peace Prize 2006 - Press Release. Retrieved from https://www.nobelprize.org/prizes/peace/2006/press-release/

Pressenza. (2024). Evolving Dhaka-Beijing ties under changing political dynamics in Bangladesh. Retrieved from https://www.pressenza.com/2024/11/evolving-dhaka-beijing-ties-under-changing-political-dynamics-in-bangladesh/

Primary Death List of ALBD. (2024). Elementary list of brutally killed leaders and activists of Bangladesh Awami League and its associated bodies. Dhaka: Bangladesh Awami League Documentation Wing.

Reuters. (2024). *Bangladesh Announces Policy Rate Rise to Combat Inflation*. Retrieved from https://www.reuters.com/world/asia-pacific/bangladesh-announces-policy-rate-rise-combat-inflation-2024-10-22/

Reuters. (2024). *Bangladesh's Yunus Hopes US Ties Will Strengthen Despite Trump Victory*. Retrieved from https://www.reuters.com/world/asia-pacific/bangladeshs-yunus-hopes-us-ties-will-strengthen-despite-trump-victory-2024-11-19.

Reuters. (2024). *Nobel laureate Muhammad Yunus was arch foe of ousted Bangladesh PM Hasina*. Retrieved from https://www.reuters.com/world/asia-pacific/nobel-laureate-muhammad-yunus-was-arch-foe-ousted-bangladesh-pm-hasina-2024-08-06/

Shehabuddin, S. (2024). *Post-1971 Challenges in Bangladesh*. Columbia University Press.

The Daily Star. (2024). *Awami League and Student Activists Unite against Interim Government*. Retrieved from https://www.thedailystar.net

The Daily Star. (2024). *Economic recovery amid supply chain disruptions*. Retrieved from https://www.thedailystar.net/business/economy/news/economic-recovery-amid-supply-chain-disruptions-3759906

The Daily Star. (2024). *Yunus Charts Path to Reforms Amid Political Upheaval*. Retrieved from https://www.thedailystar.net/news/bangladesh/news/yunus-charts-path-reforms-3700751

The Diplomat. (2024). *Bangladesh's Student Protests: A Turning Point?*. Retrieved from https://thediplomat.com/2024/07/bangladeshs-student-protests-a-turning-point/.

The Diplomat. (2024). *Can Yunus Deliver Stability in Bangladesh?*. Retrieved from https://thediplomat.com

The Diplomat. (2024). *India's Concerns over Yunus Government's Policies in Bangladesh*. Retrieved from https://thediplomat.com

The Diplomat. (2024). *Yunus' First 100 Days: Political Reforms or Consolidation of Power?*. Retrieved from https://thediplomat.com/2024/07/bangladeshs-yunus-first-100-days

The Guardian. (2024). *Global Scrutiny of Bangladesh's Interim Government Mounts*. Retrieved from https://www.theguardian.com

The Guardian. (2024). *International Criticism Grows against Yunus Government amid Rights Abuses*. Retrieved from https://www.theguardian.com

The Wall Street Journal. (2024). *Bangladesh's 'Village Banker' Faces Toughest Challenge Yet: Running His Country*. Retrieved from https://www.wsj.com/world/asia/bangladeshs-village-banker-faces-toughest-challenge-yet-running-his-country-2c1d501f

The World Bank. (2024). Strong financial sector, fiscal and monetary policy reforms will be critical to sustain Bangladesh's growth momentum. Retrieved from https://www.worldbank.org/en/news/feature/2024/04/05/strong-financial-sector-fiscal-and-monetary-policy-reforms-will-be-critical-to-sustain-bangladesh-s-growth-momentum

TIME. (2024). From 'Banker' to 'Bloodsucker': The Trials of Muhammad Yunus. Retrieved from https://time.com/6991107/muhammad-yunus-trial-sheikh-hasina-bangladesh/

Transparency International. (2024). Corruption Perceptions Index 2023. Retrieved from https://www.transparency.org/en/cpi/2023/index/bgd.

United Nations Human Rights Council. (2024). Urgent Appeal for Democratic Reforms in Bangladesh. Retrieved from https://www.ohchr.org

Violence Against Woman. (2024). Annual report on violence against women in Bangladesh. Published by the Bangladesh Hindu Buddhist Christian Unity Council.

Al-Zaman, M. S. (2019). Digital disinformation and communalism in Bangladesh. https://osf.io/preprints/socarxiv/8s6jd/download

Ferdous, A., & Huda, Z. (2023). Social media, new cultures, and new threats: impact on university students in Bangladesh. Human Behavior and

*Emerging Technologies, 2023(1), 2205861.
https://onlinelibrary.wiley.com/doi/pdf/10.1155/202
3/2205861*

*Hassan, Z. (2024). Is This the Beginning of the End
of Sheikh Hasina's Rule? Retrieved from
https://thediplomat.com/2024/07/is-this-the-
beginning-of-the-end-of-sheikh-hasinas-rule/*

*Pressxpress.px. (2024). Quota Reform: Conspiracy
behind a Movement. Retrieved from
https://pressxpress.org/2024/07/21/quota-reform-
conspiracy-behind-a-movement/*

*Rahman, T., & Jahan, I. (2020). The Role of Social
Media Rumors in Social unrest of
Bangladesh. International Journal for Studies on
Children, Women, Elderly and Disabled, 11.
https://www.ijcwed.com/wp-
content/uploads/2020/09/IJCWED11_020.pdf*

*Sharma, P, (2024, Oct 16). 'Students March with
"ISIS Flags" in Bangladesh' First Post.
https://www.google.com/amp/s/www.firstpost.com/v
antage/students-march-with-isis-flags-in-
bangladesh-vd588779/amp/*

*Al Jazeera, (2024, Aug 28). 'Bangladesh's interim
government lifts ban on Jamaat-e-Islami party'
News: Politics.
https://www.aljazeera.com/news/2024/8/28/banglad
eshs-interim-government-lifts-ban-on-jamaat-e-
islami-party*

*ANI, (2024, Oct 11). 'India "deeply disturbed" by
theft of religious article from Bangladesh temple,*

*urge authorities to investigate' Indian Narrative.
https://www.indianarrative.com/india-news/india-deeply-disturbed-by-theft-of-religious-article-from-bangladesh-temple-urge-authorities-to-investigate-163064.html 8*

*Chaudhury, D, (2024, Sep 5). 'Lawfulness prevails in Bangladesh as radical force several authorities to resign' The Economic Times.
https://m.economictimes.com/news/international/world-news/lawlessness-prevails-in-bangladesh-as-radicals-force-several-authorities-to-resign/articleshow/113101114.cms*

*Al Jazeera, (2024, Aug 5). 'Timeline: The rise and fall of Bangladesh PM Sheikh Hasina' News.
https://www.google.com/amp/s/www.aljazeera.com/amp/news/2024/8/5/timeline-sheikh-hasinas-reign-ends-after-15-years*

Akriti, A,(2024, Aug 7). 'How Bangladesh crisis may impact its economic growth: Explained' The Mint. https://www.livemint.com/economy/how-bangladesh-crisis-may-impact-its-economic-growth-explained-sheikh-hasina-muhammad-yunus-11723038572512.html

*Press Trust of India, (2024, Aug 13). 'Bangladesh's inflation spikes 12-year high to 11.66% in July amid protests' Business Standard: Dhaka.
https://www.business-standard.com/external-affairs-defence-security/news/bangladesh-s-inflation-spikes-12-year-high-to-11-66-in-july-amid-protests-124081301036_1.html*

Al Jazeera, (2024, Aug 28). 'Bangladesh's interim government lifts ban on Jamaat-e-Islami party' News: Politics. https://www.aljazeera.com/news/2024/8/28/bangladeshs-interim-government-lifts-ban-on-jamaat-e-islami-party

Hussein, A, (2024, Sep 23). 'Bangladesh Picks Up the Pieces After the Revolution' Foreign Policy: Argument. https://foreignpolicy.com/2024/09/23/bangladesh-revolution-hasina-yunus-western-relations/

TBS Report, (2024, Sep 25).' Why are the old tools of repression still in use?' The Business Standard. https://www.tbsnews.net/features/panorama/why-are-old-tools-repression-still-use-950491

Al Jazeera. (2024). Bangladesh's political crisis: What's at stake for the country's future? Retrieved from Al Jazeera

BBC News. (2024). Bangladesh: A nation at crossroads as Dr. Yunus takes charge. Retrieved from BBC News

Chatham House. (2024). Sheikh Hasina's departure exposes fractures in Bangladesh's politics. https://www.chathamhouse.org/2024/08/sheikh-hasinas-departure-exposes-fractures-bangladeshs-politics

Guardian News and Media. (2024). Bangladesh now angles toward a Taliban-style regime. South Asia Guardian. https://slguardian.org/bangladesh-now-angles-toward-a-taliban-style-

regime/?fbclid=IwZXh0bgNhZW0CMTEAAR1hoY9
gFBQojlz6RMmPStwpKY07XHUvrJ3p-kDs0T-
GLB9feWhJ72r2fps_aem__8DKaxQlZZCH3CMrxfc
ilw

The Nobel Prize. (2006). The Nobel Peace Prize
2006 - Muhammad Yunus, Grameen Bank.
Retrieved from The Nobel Prize Official Website